A future ONLY God can See FOR You

A GUIDE FOR TEEN AND YOUNG ADULT WOMEN ON PREPARING TO LEAD

SUSAN R. MADSEN

CFI

An imprint of Cedar Fort, Inc.

Springville, Utah

ISBN 13: 978–1–4621–4052-7

Published by CFI, an imprint of Cedar Fort, Inc.
2373 W. 700 S., Springville, UT, 84663
Distributed by Cedar Fort, Inc., www.cedarfort.com

Library of Congress Control Number: 2021946174

Cover design by Courtney Proby
Cover design © 2021 Cedar Fort, Inc.

Printed in the United States of America

10 9 8 7 6 5 4 3 2 1

Printed on acid-free paper

For my daughter, granddaughter, nieces, and grandnieces

SCHOLARLY BOOKS
BY THIS AUTHOR

Handbook of Research on Gender and Leadership (2017)

Women and Leadership around the World (2015)

Women as Global Leaders (2015)

Women and Leadership in Higher Education (2014)

*Developing Leadership: Learning from the
Experiences of Women Governors* (2008)

*On Becoming a Woman Leader: Learning from the
Experiences of University Presidents* (2008)

CONTENTS

CONTENTS

ACKNOWLEDGMENTS

I owe a great deal of gratitude to many people who have encouraged and supported my work through the years.

I am grateful to my parents (Boyd and Helen Willden) who laid the foundation for my faith, faithfulness, and commitment to the Lord and His work.

My children (Michael, Brian, Staci, and Scott) for helping me grow and develop Christlike attributes through the years. My daughter-in-law (Carlee) for her insights and my son-in-law (Craig) for his encouragement. My grandchildren (Parks and Hadley) for the joy they bring to me. My six brothers who have always been a steady source of love and encouragement (Dave, Mark, Doug, Lynn, Tim, and Stephen). And particularly, my brother (Tim Willden) for his deep insight and understanding of the love the Lord has for women and the role they need to play in the Church in the years ahead.

My research assistant for this book, Allie Barnes, for her work and insight. For Heather Sundahl and Robbyn Scribner, who provided wonderful feedback and suggestions. And to my friend and department head at Utah State University, Jim Davis, for his remarkable support.

And finally, I am grateful to my husband, Greg, for his constant support and encouragement to do what I feel God has called me to do.

PREFACE

Almost daily people ask me why I work so hard to strengthen the impact of girls and women in Utah, the United States, and around the world. I always answer the same way—because I feel called to do so. As a committed, covenant-keeping member of The Church of Jesus Christ of Latter-day Saints, I believe that it is absolutely critical to accomplish the work that God has planned for us to do on earth. I feel both the weight and the blessing of that call. I also believe this work is a gift, as I am able to do work that gives me a deep sense of purpose.

Parker J. Palmer, a well-known educator and author, writes beautifully about wholeness, calling, and listening. A quote from his book *Let Your Life Speak* has stuck with me for many years: "Before you tell your life what you intend to do with it, listen for what it intends to do with you. Before you tell your life what truths and values you have decided to live up to, let your life tell you what truths you embody, what values you represent."[1] This is what I've tried to do—to let the Savior guide my life.

This book is one of many projects I have felt called to do, and I have loved the journey. Writing is not an easy process, but through the process of reflecting, wrestling, and writing, the words have come. I have been so inspired as I have reread all the fabulous quotes that I have collected over the years from Church leaders. I've felt guided by the Spirit as I have brought my whole self to this project, and I have felt joy when the words and concepts have connected in ways that I believe will help girls and women in the Church today.

---

1. Palmer, *Let Your Life Speak*, 3.

This book is about preparing teen and young adult women to become leaders. I don't say this lightly. I truly believe that we must have more women in the Church strengthen their confidence, use their voices, and become leaders in their homes, neighborhoods, schools, universities, businesses, governments, states, regions, and countries. Things are changing, and this is more important today than ever before in the history of the world. We are needed, and the time is now. To the girls and women reading this book, I hope you will find knowledge, motivation, inspiration, and courage to step out of your comfort zone to become the daughter of God He needs you to become in these last days. Our Heavenly Parents are depending on us.

Let's begin.

INTRODUCTION

"I am a beloved daughter of heavenly parents, with a divine nature and eternal destiny."

—YOUNG WOMEN THEME[1]

We are told that we have Heavenly Parents who have a plan for each of us, yet most of us struggle to know what that might look like. We are told we are daughters of God, yet many of us wrestle to understand what that really means. We are told that we have unique talents, gifts, and strengths, but often we don't understand how we could be different from the billions of other girls and women who live or have lived on this earth. We are told we have a special purpose, yet often that purpose is hard to decipher. But I need you to know, I believe all we have been taught. In fact, I don't just believe it—I know it!

Elder Dieter F. Uchtdorf of the Quorum of the Twelve Apostles once said, "God sent you here to prepare for a future greater than anything you can imagine. . . . God knows of your successes. . . . He knows of the times you have held onto the fading light and believed—even in the midst of growing darkness. He knows of your sufferings. He knows of your remorse for the times you have fallen short or failed. And he still loves you. . . . He loves you not only for who you are . . . but also for the person of glory and light you have the potential. . . to become."[2]

---

1. "Young Women Theme," para. 1.
2. Uchtdorf, "Living the Gospel Joyful," 121.

1

So, can you trust that God sees a future for you that is greater than anything you can imagine? Can you trust that He loves you for who you are? Can you trust that your Heavenly Parents see amazing potential for who you can become? Yes! It's true. You *can* trust and believe. Because when you can trust, really trust, in your Heavenly Parents and their Son, things will change for you. When you can let His trust and His love totally wash over you, you will know that you need to prepare for a future only God can see for you.

Former Young Women General President Elaine Dalton has stated that sisters in this church have been prepared and reserved to be on the earth now.[3] Yet, evil forces around us work hard to decrease our sense of self-worth, increase the messages that we are not good enough, and diminish our beliefs that we have unlimited potential. As women of faith, we know better. But do we truly believe? And do we make our daily choices based on these beliefs?

I have been concerned for years about a gap in the Church between *hearing* and *reciting* the truths taught versus actually *believing* and *knowing* them. For example, we often hear the message that we are daughters of Heavenly Parents with a divine nature and inherent worth. This focuses on what is truly important—internal attributes. Yet, we know that many girls and women have been conditioned to be incredibly preoccupied with their external appearance. In fact, Utah (the state I live in) is well-known for extremely high levels (per capita) of spending on hair coloring, cosmetics and skin-care products, minimally invasive cosmetic procedures (such as Botox injections), and more invasive types of elective plastic surgery.[4] Although this is just one example, it is a struggle that is seen around the world as well.

As women in this Church, we must remember that "the worth of souls is great in the sight of God" (D&C 18:10) but that "the Lord uses a scale very different from the world's to weigh the worth

---

3. Dalton, *No Ordinary Women*, 53–54.
4. Madsen, Dillon, and Scribner, "Cosmetic Surgery and Body Image among Utah Women."

of a soul."[5] Despite worldly pressures to focus on outward appearance, it is who we are on the inside that matters to our Savior. In her book *No Ordinary Women*, President Dalton said, "We are daughters of God. We are not ordinary women. We were born to be leaders . . . [and] we have a great work to do."[6]

We all know people who seem "born to be leaders"—people who are confident and outgoing, people who are sure of themselves and comfortable commanding large crowds. These can be characteristics of good leaders, but there are many ways to lead. If you can learn to speak up and stand for truth, you can be a leader. If you can influence those around you through quiet persuasion and example, you can be a leader. In later chapters I will explore the many ways and numerous reasons women can claim their right to lead and influence and teach you how to develop your own personal style. But for now, know that President Dalton is right—you have a great work to do!

Why am I writing this book? The quick answer is that I feel called to do so. I have been studying, teaching, and writing about women's leadership for decades. This includes researching the lifetime development of leadership in top women leaders around the world. I have learned so much about how to raise girls to become more confident, use their voices, and step into roles of influence. Although most of my work has not been within the context of The Church of Jesus Christ of Latter-day Saints, it all relates. In fact, when I speak to girls and women who have the gospel of Jesus Christ in their lives—no matter where in the world I am—the Spirit witnesses to me every time that each of us needs to prepare to lead.

My hope is that teen and young adult women from all walks of life will read this book. This includes those who want a fuller understanding of their purpose and calling and those who want to take a deeper dive into their own unique talents, gifts, and strengths. If you are reading this, I expect you already yearn to contribute in new and

---

5. Uchtdorf, "You Matter to Him," 22.
6. Dalton, *No Ordinary Women*, 21, 53.

different ways in various types of settings—home, church, schools, colleges, businesses, nonprofits, or the community. Yet, you may have received mixed messages about the role of women in the Church, and some of you may wonder if your yearnings are even "right." I expect many of you do not yet feel prepared to influence in the ways you envision and want to strengthen your confidence. Some of you may want to increase your sense of self-worth or understand what the Church teaches on many of these topics. Or maybe you are looking for confirmation that God needs your unique gifts and that you can and should do important work inside and outside the home. If any of these resonate, this book is for you. It is for anyone interested in becoming better, stronger, and more confident. It is for anyone who wants to find more joy and purpose in their lives.

To help you on your journey, I have designed and divided this book into four parts. In part I, I discuss why preparing to influence and lead is so important. To do this, I set the stage by helping you understand why God needs you to lead (chapter 1), describing what leadership is about (chapter 2), outlining the benefits of having women in leadership roles and on leadership teams (chapter 3), and highlighting the wide variety of ways and places you can influence and lead (chapter 4).

In part II, I focus on how you can prepare yourself for leadership. Using both research and Church teachings and doctrine as the foundation for these chapters, I discuss how you can strengthen your confidence (chapter 5), discover your gifts, talents, and strengths (chapter 6), learn about mindsets (chapter 7), pursue learning and education (chapter 8), explore your purpose and callings (chapter 9), and understand your identity (chapter 10).

Continuing, in part III I will share content that will help you wrestle with some of the challenges you might face along your leadership preparation journey. These include understanding the shadow side of social media (chapter 11), exploring the complexity of body image (chapter 12), recognizing mental health struggles (chapter 13), and grappling with mixed messages (chapter 14).

And finally, part IV will wrap the book up by providing some ideas and insights on how you should consider moving forward.

Don't worry, I won't tell you what to do! However, I will offer some perspectives and tools that may be useful in your journey. To do this, the final two chapters include unleashing the power of personal revelation (chapter 15) and taking the road less traveled (chapter 16). I have also created an associated workbook that you can use, alongside this book, to help you get the most out of what you are learning. (It's called *A Future Only God Can See for You: A Workbook for Teen and Young Adult Women on Preparing to Lead*.)

This is your time to prepare to make a difference. As President Dalton proclaimed, "We are not here to sit back and be passive. We are here to lead. . . . Live a purposeful life, not a passive life. Arise!"[7] President Thomas S. Monson told the women of the Church over a decade ago, "You are a mighty force for good, one of the most powerful in the entire world."[8] And, I would add, we *are* a mighty force, but we *must* be prepared to do more!

In the words of renowned poet Etienne de Grillet, "I shall pass through this world but once. If therefore, there be any kindness I can show, or any good thing I can do, let me do it now: let me not defer or neglect it, for I shall not pass this way again."[9]

No matter where you are on life's pathway, my hope is that this book will inspire you, motivate you, challenge you, and propel you forward in your journey to influence and lead; that you will emerge with a stronger belief that God needs you to prepare for leadership in your homes, churches, communities, and beyond; and that now is the time to begin building the future that only God can see for you.

---

7. Ibid., 22.
8. Monson, "Three Goals to Guide You," 120.
9. Grellet, "Etienne de Grellet Quotes."

PART I

Leadership

CHAPTER 1

God Needs You

"Part of the tragedy you must avoid is to discover too late that you missed an opportunity to prepare for a future only God could see for you."[1]

—PRESIDENT HENRY B. EYRING

God needs you to prepare now to become a leader. This statement might sound a bit strong to some of you, but I believe it with all my soul. Why? Because I hear it from two sources: Church leaders and directly from my Heavenly Father. In this chapter, I make a case for the first. I'll provide many statements and teachings that will help you consider more deeply the role that covenant-keeping women have today and in the years and decades ahead. But you'll need to do the second part yourself. This book will guide you along that path, but it is ultimately up to you to receive that confirmation and guidance from your Heavenly Father.

Personal revelation on these concepts and principles may come quickly if you welcome the Spirit as you read and ponder, but it could also take more time and work than you expect. Each of you has a path of growth that will be unlike your friends' or any other

---

1. Eyring, "Education for Real Life," 18.

woman's. The path you will take is only yours, but you don't have to walk it alone. Talk about what you are reading with your friends, Young Women leaders, parents, and even the sisters you minister to. I promise that personal revelation will come if you do your part. And I hope you learn to recognize the whisperings of the Spirit in new ways. Spiritual moments matter.

A year after inspired changes were made to the Young Women program, the Young Women General Presidency shared the following reflection on November 5, 2020, in the *Church News*: "Heavenly Father loves all of His young daughters all over the world, and He sees them as young women who are exercising faith in Jesus Christ. As time goes on, they will continue to be women of God, knowing how to serve, lead, love and minister in Christ's holy name."[2] The path is being prepared for you to serve. What a choice time to learn to "serve, lead, love and minister."

CHANGE IS ALL AROUND US

In his powerful 2015 general conference talk titled "A Plea to My Sisters," President Russell M. Nelson made a statement that I think about often: "It would be impossible to measure the influence that such women have, not only on families but also on the Lord's Church, as wives, mothers, and grandmothers; as sisters and aunts; as teachers and leaders; and especially as exemplars and devout defenders of the faith. This has been true in every gospel dispensation since the days of Adam and Eve. **Yet the women of this dispensation are distinct from the women of any other because this dispensation is distinct from any other**. This distinction brings both privileges and responsibilities."[3]

President Nelson is saying that women in the Church right now are distinct from women who have lived on this earth at any other time. It is a different time and a different world. We have different temptations and different challenges. We need to be prepared in different ways for

---

2.   "Young Women General Presidency: 'What's in a Name?'" in *Church News*.
3.   Nelson, "A Plea to My Sisters," 95–96, emphasis added.

different opportunities. This book will explore what all that means for teen and young adult women today. Our homes, schools, universities, workplaces, communities, and governments are different than they used to be. However, "different" doesn't mean bad; it just means different. As you may remember, President Nelson has also encouraged us to take our vitamins and get some rest because exciting days are ahead.[4]

The Church of Jesus Christ of Latter-day Saints is also changing. Although doctrines remain consistent, policies and practices are changing more quickly than ever before. In 2014, Elder David A. Bednar of the Quorum of the Twelve Apostles said, "If the Lord is hastening His work, we cannot keep doing things the same way we have always done them."[5] He was right. In recent years, we have seen so many changes in Church policies and practices that directly impact women. Consider these examples:

- 2012: Sister missionaries began serving at age nineteen instead of having to wait until they are twenty-one.
- 2013: The role of Sister Training Leader was created for sister missionaries, and these leaders were invited to attend the newly formed Mission Leadership Council.
- 2017: It was announced that both the women and priesthood sessions at general conference would be held annually (instead of priesthood sessions being held more often).
- 2018: Visiting teaching was changed to ministering, and young women were included in those assignments.
- 2018: The First Presidency updated missionary dress and grooming standards, which included the opportunity for sister missionaries to wear pants.
- 2019: The temple ceremony language was changed to be more inclusive to women.
- 2021: Girls and women who have been baptized began serving as witnesses for baptisms. Sisters began serving as

---

4. "President Nelson About the Church in the Coming Years: 'Eat Your Vitamin Pills. Get Some Rest. It's Going to Be Exciting,'" in *LDS Living*.
5. "Apostle Instructs Hundreds in Uganda," in *Newsroom*.

witnesses in the temple for baptisms (including limited-use recommends) and sealings (endowed members).

- 2019: A new Young Women theme, class name, and structure changes were announced.
- 2021: The position of international area organization advisors for sisters was created.
- 2021: Saturday evening women and priesthood sessions of general conference were dissolved. The Saturday evening session is now for a general audience.

Of course, many foundational elements of the Church are consistent and unchanging, but some shifts are important for the growth of the Church. And all of them impact you.

Finally, in her book *Women and the Priesthood*, Sheri L. Dew said: "I believe that the moment we learn to unleash the full influence of converted, covenant-keeping women, the kingdom of God will change overnight."[6] This includes converted, covenant-keeping young women too! Isn't this powerful?

So, let's summarize: President Nelson said that women today are distinct from the women of any other dispensation, Elder Bednar told us that we cannot keep doing things the same way we have always done them, and Sister Dew proclaimed that things will change overnight when converted, covenant-keeping women are unleashed. The time is now, and you need to be prepared to influence in ways women in the Church have never done before. Are you ready to get started? I hope so!

POWERFUL GUIDANCE

When I share the words of Church leaders in firesides around the world, sisters often tell me that the encouragement I give is new to them. One of my brothers has been a stake president for many years, and I remember early in his tenure he asked me to speak at a fireside for the women in his stake. Afterward, he told me that

---

6.   Dew, *Women and the Priesthood*, 163.

a sister from his stake came up to him and said, "President Will-den, do you really believe and support what Sister Madsen spoke about this evening?" He responded, "With all my heart," and then discussed how I shared the teachings of Church leaders to support everything I said. She paused and then asked, "Will you please tell my husband?" The information I share may be new to some members of the Church, but the guidance of Church leaders on this topic is clear and has been for some time. Here are several of my favorite quotes through the decades that will help you better understand why God needs you to prepare to influence and lead:

> It is not for you to be led by the women of the world; it is for you to lead the . . . women of the world, in everything that is praiseworthy, everything that is God-like, everything that is uplifting and . . . purifying to the children of men.
>
> —President Joseph F. Smith (1914)[7]

> Much of the major growth that is coming to the Church in the last days will come because many of the good women of the world (in whom there is often such an inner sense of spirituality) will be drawn to the Church in large numbers. This will happen to the degree that the women of the Church reflect righteousness and articulateness in their lives and to the degree that the women of the Church are seen as distinct and different—in happy ways—from the women of the world.
>
> —President Spencer W. Kimball (1979)[8]

> I have often thought that if great numbers of the women of all nations were to unite and lift up their voices in the cause of peace, there would develop a worldwide will for peace which could save our civilization and avoid untold suffering, misery, plague, starvation, and the death of millions.
>
> —President Gordon B. Hinckley (1985)[9]

I plead with my sisters of The Church of Jesus Christ of Latter-day Saints to step forward! Take your rightful and needful place in your

---

7. *Teachings of Presidents of the Church: Joseph F. Smith*, 184.
8. Kimball, "The Role of Righteous Women, para. 24.
9. Hinckley, "Ten Gifts from the Lord," para. 10.

home, in your community, and in the kingdom of God—more than you ever have before. . . . [I] bless you [dear sisters] to rise to your full stature, to fulfill the measure of your creation, as we walk arm in arm in this sacred work.

—President Russell M. Nelson (2015)[10]

We are uniquely positioned in a changing and challenging time to serve others and contribute in such a way that our righteous influence will literally change the world. We must go forward with full confidence. . . . Who knows but that we each have 'come to the kingdom for such a time as this' and are even now being polished by our challenges?

—President Elaine Dalton (2016)[11]

These passages from Church leaders clearly state that committed and covenant-keeping women today are needed to 1) lead the women of the world in righteous ways; 2) influence by being spiritual, happy, distinct, and different; 3) develop a worldwide will for peace; 4) step forward in the home, community, and kingdom of God; and 5) change the world through service and leadership. All these elements require action, and all these elements require leadership. Can you see why I have no doubt that each of you needs to be prepared to lead?

CHARACTERISTICS AND ACTIONS

I mentioned at the beginning of this chapter that I would share statements and teachings from Church leaders that will help you consider more deeply the role that covenant-keeping women will need to take in the years and decades ahead. And I wasn't kidding! I am setting the stage for the rest of the book by helping you understand that women can and should be leaders. I want to continue by sharing five more quotes and highlighting specific leadership characteristics and actions that are needed by women today (notice the italicized words I want to emphasize).

First, in a worldwide leadership training, President Gordon B. Hinckley stated: "It is so tremendously important that the women of the Church *stand strong and immovable* for that which is correct

---

10. Nelson, "A Plea to My Sisters," 97.
11. Dalton, *No Ordinary Women*, 43.

and proper under the plan of the Lord. . . . If they will *be united* and *speak with one voice* their strength will be incalculable. We call upon the women of the Church to *stand together* for righteousness. They must begin in their own homes. They can *teach it* in their classes. They can *voice it* in their communities."[12]

Second, in a speech to Saints in 2014 at the Uganda Kampala Stake Center in Kologo, Elder David A. Bednar taught that when *women become more equal partners with men*, the Lord will hasten His work, but *equal does not mean identical*.[13]

Third, in a 2015 general conference address, Young Women General President Bonnie L. Oscarson proclaimed: "Let us help build the kingdom of God by *standing up boldly* and *being defenders* of marriage, parenthood, and the home. The Lord needs us to be *brave, steadfast, and immovable warriors* who will *defend* His plan and *teach* the upcoming generations His truths."[14]

Fourth, in 1992, President Howard W. Hunter said the following: "It seems to me that there is a great need to rally the women of the Church to *stand with* and for the Brethren in stemming the tide of evil that surrounds us and in *moving forward the work* of our Savior. . . . So we entreat you to minister with your *powerful influence* for good in *strengthening our families, our church, and our communities*."[15]

And finally, President Russell M. Nelson made the following declaration: "We . . . need your *strength*, your *conversion*, your *conviction*, your *ability to lead*, your *wisdom*, and your *voices*. The kingdom of God is not and cannot be complete without women who make *sacred covenants* and then keep them, women who can *speak with the power and authority of God!*"[16]

Let me make sense of these five quotes and the words I have italicized. What exactly are young women and women in this Church being asked to do? Check out this list and see what you think:

12. *Daughters in My Kingdom*, 160; emphasis added.
13. "Apostle Instructs Hundreds in Uganda," in *Newsroom*; emphasis added.
14. Oscarson, "Defenders of the Family Proclamation," 17; emphasis added.
15. Hunter, "To the Women of the Church," para. 14; emphasis added.
16. Nelson, "A Plea to My Sisters," 96; emphasis added.

- Be brave.
- Be converted.
- Be defenders.
- Be immovable warriors.
- Be steadfast.
- Be united.
- Become equal partners.
- Defend His plan.
- Have conviction.
- Impart wisdom.
- Make and keep sacred covenants.
- Minister with powerful influence.
- Speak with one voice.
- Speak with the power and authority of God.
- Stand strong and immovable.
- Stand together.
- Stand up boldly.
- Stand with and for Church leaders.
- Strengthen our communities.
- Strengthen our families.
- Strengthen the Church.
- Teach gospel truths.
- Teach righteousness.
- Use your ability to lead.
- Use your voice.

Now, if we are being asked to *do* these things, then what are we also being asked to *become*? **We are being asked to become leaders**. All the things we've been asked to "do" are leadership activities and characteristics. Believe me, I'm a leadership professor and have been teaching university courses for years. In past decades, many women in the Church have felt discounted or silenced, and unfortunately, there have been situations where I have felt that way myself. But this is not God's plan. **God needs women to lead. Period.**

CONCLUSION

Our Heavenly Parents, who know each of you perfectly, have reserved you to come to earth at this specific time in the history of the world. They knew that the stakes would be higher and the opposition would be more intense than ever before.[17] Yet, they chose you to come now for very specific reasons. I don't know the reasons, and you probably don't either, but they will become clear as you move forward on a purposeful path of preparation. The challenges you face and the opportunities you create and receive are intentionally designed to refine you so that you can prepare to influence in ways no one else can.[18] And there is no other time in the history of the world that we as women have been faced with "greater complexity in [our] concerns."[19] According to Sheri L. Dew, former counselor in the General Relief Society Presidency, "We are living in a day unlike any other, which means it is time for us to do things we have never done before."[20] And, as one recent *Ensign* article taught, women in the Church "individually and as a united whole, are needed to lead, not follow, the world."[21]

To paraphrase Winston Churchill, former prime minister of the United Kingdom (replacing "man" and "his" with "woman" and "her"): "To every *woman* there comes in *her* lifetime that special moment when *she* is figuratively tapped on the shoulder and offered the chance to do a special thing, unique to *her* and fitted to *her* talents. What a tragedy if that moment finds *her* unprepared or unqualified for the work which would be *her* finest hour."[22] Our Heavenly Parents need you more than ever before, as young women and adults in The Church of Jesus Christ of Latter-day Saints, to become prepared to step forward and lead in your homes, church congregations, communities, and beyond.

---

17. Reeder and Holbrook (eds), *At the Pulpit*, 269.
18. Dalton, *No Ordinary Women*, 43.
19. Holland, "One Thing Needful," para. 11.
20. Dew, *Amazed by Grace*, 60.
21. Gardner, "Connecting Daughters of God with His Priesthood Power," 37.
22. Churchill, "A Man's Finest Hour," para. 1.

CHAPTER 2
Leadership Described

"Each time a [person] stands up for an ideal, or acts
to improve the lot of others, or strikes out against
injustice, [s]he sends forth a tiny ripple of hope, and
crossing each other from a million different centers of
energy and daring those ripples build a current that
can sweep down the mightiest walls of oppression
and resistance."[1]

—ROBERT F. KENNEDY

To many people, leadership in today's world looks loud, forceful, uncompromising, selfish, closed-minded, dishonest, and egotistical. Yet, that is not what effective leadership is about. I agree with Sheryl Sandberg, chief operating officer of Facebook, who said, "Leadership is not bullying and leadership is not aggression. Leadership is the expectation that you can use your voice for good. That you can make the world a better place."[2] When you think about leadership in this way, I expect you can better see yourself as the leader you want to become. Always remember that *you* can choose how *you* influence, impact, and lead.

---

1. Kennedy, "Day of Affirmation Address."
2. Starr, "Sheryl Sandberg wants to ban the word 'bossy,'" para. 7.

In this chapter, I will help you better understand what leadership is. That might sound simple, but it is more complex than you would think. Your perceptions about leaders and leadership can directly impact your aspirations and ambitions to influence. Shifting previously held beliefs can empower you to imagine yourself serving and impacting in ways you may not have imagined before. And, as I have said before, you need to imagine and dream of that future only God can see for you.

DEFINITIONS

To prepare to become a leader, it is important that you understand what leadership is and how it might look. There are thousands of definitions of leadership, but the one I use the most is the following: "Leadership is a process whereby an individual influences a group of individuals to achieve a common goal."[3] There are four main elements in this definition: 1) it is a process, 2) where an individual influences, 3) a group of people, and 4) toward a common goal. That's it. If you are doing these four things in any situation, you *are* leading and therefore you *are* a leader.

For example, you may be asked to plan and coordinate a two-hour service project one evening for a youth or young single adult activity. Your efforts are a *process* because there are a series of steps and actions that you will put into motion. You are also *influencing* because you are planning something that *a group of people* will participate in, and your activity has a *goal*—to serve one or more people. This is leadership.

When I speak about leadership, I often use the words *impact* and *influence* as well. To positively impact someone means to influence, to use power, to affect, to persuade, to sway, to have a strong effect on, and to lead. The word *influence* is defined as the power or capacity to cause an effect, a compelling force, an alteration, and an action or process of effecting actions, behaviors, or opinions of others. These two words are focused on action and, depending on

---

3. Northouse, *Leadership: Theory and practice* (8th edition), 5.

my audience, I often use these two interchangeably with leadership. Believe it or not, sometimes girls and women tune me out when I use the word *leadership*.

ATTRIBUTES

Many great leaders have lived on this earth throughout the centuries, but the greatest of all was our Savior. President Spencer W. Kimball taught, "We will find it very difficult to be significant leaders unless we recognize the reality of the perfect leader, Jesus Christ, and let him be the light by which we see the way!"[4] Although there are many ways to lead, our Savior was the most remarkable role model for each of us. He led by example. He led with humility. He gave people a purpose. Doctrine and Covenants 4:6 highlights some of the characteristics of the Savior's divine character: "Remember faith, virtue, knowledge, temperance, patience, brotherly kindness, godliness, charity, humility, diligence."

These are all attributes of leaders who transform followers in Christlike ways, though they are not characteristics we necessarily associate with leadership. But great, even Christlike, leadership looks different depending on the person, situation, setting, or circumstance. For example, Elder M. Russell Ballard of the Quorum of the Twelve Apostles said to the sisters, "Be bold. Be assertive. Feel confident about raising weighty issues and concerns. You have as much right to input and inspiration as other . . . members."[5]

And, as former Young Women General President Bonnie L. Oscarson declared, "We need to boldly defend the Lord's revealed doctrines describing marriage, families, the divine roles of men and women, and the importance of homes as sacred places—even when the world is shouting in our ears that these principles are outdated, limiting, or no longer relevant."[6]

---

4. Kimball, "Jesus: The Perfect Leader," para. 34.
5. Ballard, *Counseling with Our Councils*, 102.
6. Oscarson, "Defenders of the Family Proclamation," 15.

Christlike leadership *can* be bold, assertive, vocal, persistent, persuasive, and determined. It can also be unspoken, soft-spoken, selfless, calm, and unwavering. In fact, sometimes it can be a combination of all of these.

In discussing positive historical leaders, I want to highlight two women as well. The first is Mother Teresa, who was nun, a charity worker in India, and a powerful role model and amazing leader. Mother Teresa had a clear vision, founded Missionaries of Charity in India, and worked for forty-five years looking after the poor, sick, orphaned, and dying. She was a selfless servant leader who dedicated her whole life to making others' lives better. Teresa won the Nobel Peace Prize in 1979 and India's highest civilian honor in 1980 for her humanitarian work. She had vision, dedication, persistence, determination, and was committed to a cause—all critical leadership attributes.

The other is Sister Eliza R. Snow, who was a pioneer, an early president of the Relief Society, president of Deseret Hospital, president of the Women's Department of the Endowment House, and a poet and author. She was opinionated, vocal, feisty, bold, candid, persuasive, artistic, intelligent, and wise. She was opinionated, vocal, feisty, bold, candid, persuasive, artistic, intelligent, and wise. Sister Snow was authentic and used these attributes to lead boldly in the early days of the Church. She was a powerful force for good, and her poems, minutes, and other writings are still used today.

Although I mentioned some of the traits, characteristics, or attributes of these three leaders, *leadership* is about *action*. If you study the *actions* of the three leaders I just highlighted in more depth, you'll find that their leadership efforts include *processes* (steps and actions that you will put into motion) and *influencing groups of people* (by inspiring and persuading in different ways) toward a *common goal*. For Christ, that goal was to save souls; for Mother Teresa it was to help the poor, sick, orphaned, and dying; and for Eliza R. Snow it was to move the work of the Lord forward.

While it is inspiring and instructive to study the lives of leaders whose actions have affected many, we must always remember that leadership can also happen in small and simple ways. Leadership can be coordinating a family home evening, teaching a Young Women lesson, inviting a family in your neighborhood to come to church, or being the first to walk away from an offensive joke or situation. Leadership can happen in moments. Leadership can happen anywhere.

CHARACTERISTICS

As a professor, I teach a leadership course nearly every semester, and a favorite activity of mine is putting students into groups of four to six and giving them a stack of 100 sticky notes and two markers. I ask them to write down any words they can think of (one word or phrase on each sticky note) when I say the words *leader* or *leadership*. It is a competition between groups to see how many words they can come up with in a short period of time, and we stop when most of the groups finish their 100. I have the students put the sticky notes up on whiteboards and walls around the room and ask the class to make sense of what they see. They then work to move the notes into categories and themes so we can all examine what surfaced. I admit that it sometimes gets crazy with sticky notes flying around the room and some students stepping back because the chaos can be overwhelming, but the activity provides the foundation for a remarkable conversation to help us start off the semester.

Typically, what emerges from this activity is a long list of traits, skills, behaviors, and other types of characteristics:

- *Traits* typically include things people are born with—personality characteristics—such as height, intelligence, extraversion, self-confidence, determination, sociability, responsibility, cooperativeness, masculinity, motivation, drive, appearance, assertiveness, and dominance.
- *Skills*—the leader's capabilities that can be learned—include characteristics like problem-solving, understanding people, planning, visioning, organizing, technical aptitudes, and learning new material, among many others.
- *Behaviors*—what leaders do and how they act—often include things like communicating, listening, delegating,

directing, coaching, supporting, guiding, involving, engaging, controlling, dictating, bossing, and clarifying.

Yet there is so much more to leadership than the traits you were born with, the skills you have learned, and the behaviors you currently display. I'll discuss this in more depth in later chapters.

Interestingly, in nearly all cases (unless I'm facilitating a women-only workshop) the themes that emerge from this sticky note activity look very masculine—the way leadership has looked throughout time. In fact, in research studies when people of all ages are asked to draw a picture of a leader, the results are almost always the same in terms of gender. Boys, girls, men, and women all draw a man.[7] This is because leadership is still viewed by most people in the world as a masculine trait or activity. However, as I will discuss in chapter 3, the more feminine leadership characteristics are those that are now being shown to be incredibly effective in today's world. But I want to warn you (although it's probably not a surprise) that most people still view men as leaders and women as supporters and followers.

In fact, girls and women often run into what is called a "double-bind," which is a statement or concept that has two elements that contrast with each other. Because leaders are still viewed as masculine (strong, decisive, assertive) and most people expect women to be feminine (nurturing, emotional, communicative, selfless), it is often hard for women to be seen as leaders. So, when women are strong, decisive, assertive, and take charge, they can be viewed as *competent*, but they are also *disliked*. And when women display their feminine qualities, they are *liked* but viewed as *less competent*. Often, when a woman behaves in as stereotypically masculine way, people wonder what is wrong with her. And when a woman behaves how a woman is expected to behave, she is not viewed as a leader.[8] Most of this is happening below the surface. It is often unconscious and based on our upbringings and societal norms. This is one of the reasons you don't

---

7. Murphy, "Picture a Leader. Is She a Woman?"
8. Catalyst, "Infographic: The Double-Bind Dilemma for Women in Leadership."

see as many women in leadership roles. I know this is a bit of a downer (sorry about that), but you need to know. The good news is that things are changing. There is hope, and as I clearly outlined in chapter 1, the Lord needs you to embrace your divine role as a leader.

Overall, the way you lead will be individual and unique. You can watch and learn about leaders of all kinds in many different settings. You can observe and reflect on both the good and bad examples of leaders and leadership around you. However, I always advise that you do not try to become exactly like anyone else. You have and can build your own unique leadership style, which will shift, change, and become refined as you learn, grow, and expand with experience. And, integrating and developing the positive attributes you see in others can help. Yet, you will need to find your own authentic approach that positively impacts others in the best ways possible.

CONCLUSION

This chapter has focused on describing what leadership is and how it can be displayed by different leaders in distinctive ways. Through considering the leadership definitions, attributes, and characteristics I have discussed in this chapter, I hope that you can better understand what leadership might look like for you.

Using your voice *is* being a leader. Your voice matters. I love this quote by Pakistani activist Malala Yousafzai: "When the whole world is silent, even one voice becomes powerful."[9] I would add that even when the whole world is noisy, one voice can still be powerful. And that voice can be yours. American writer and civil rights activist Audre Lorde also stated, "When we speak, we are afraid our words will not be heard or welcomed. But when we are silent, we are still afraid. So, it is better to speak." Speaking up and using your voice in positive ways can change lives.

In the early days of the Church, Sister Eliza R. Snow explained that it was high time to rise up in the "dignity of our calling and

---

9.   Yousafzaim, "Quotable Quote."

speak for ourselves." She said, "The world does not know us, and truth and justice to our brethren and to ourselves demands us to speak. . . . We are not inferior to the ladies of the world, and we do not want to appear so."[10] If you are going to fulfill this responsibility, each of you needs to prepare yourself to find and use your voice and then be ready to step forward to influence and impact. You need to be ready to lead tomorrow, next year, and for the rest of your life!

10. *Daughters in My Kingdom*, 47.

CHAPTER 3

The Benefits of Women Leaders

"It is only when both perspectives come together that the picture is balanced and complete. Men and women are equally valuable in the ongoing work of the gospel kingdom"[1]

—ELDER M. RUSSELL BALLARD

Joan Chittister, author and Roman Catholic nun, once stated: "Without the input of women, humanity sees with only one eye, hears with only one ear and thinks with only one half of the human mind."[2] In my work, I've found that most people don't understand the value of having both women and men serve together in leadership teams. Through the years, more times than I would like to admit, I've had people tell me that it doesn't matter if women lead because, as one woman stated, "It just matters that leaders are good people." This statement may seem reasonable, but that fact is that having leaders of each gender *does* matter. It matters a lot! In fact, a

---

1. Ballard, *Counseling with Our Councils*, 103.
2. Chittister, "We Are at a Crossroads for Women in the Church," para. 17.

ton of research supports this, and it is true in all settings, including families, church congregations, communities, political bodies, businesses, nonprofit entities, and educational institutions.

In this chapter I will help you recognize the benefits of having women in key positions of influence. It is important for women to lead. When groups, teams, organizations, and societies are more thoughtful in terms of getting the right combination of people in leadership roles, the best decisions can be made. And we need better decisions in our world today!

BETTER TOGETHER

Studies continue to show that more gender-diverse leadership teams—teams with men *and* women—are more creative and innovative. A leadership team can take many forms, including parents in a home, ward youth councils, city councils or state legislatures, or nonprofit boards of directors. You may wonder, "Why is more creativity and innovation important to leadership teams?" There are so many complex challenges in the world today that we are in constant need of answers to both ongoing and new problems. To do this, we need a mix of diverse minds to design effective solutions. Problem-solving is a critical skill for any leader in today's world.

Decades of research from organizational scientists, psychologists, sociologists, economists, and others have agreed that we must have both men and women in teams and organizations to enhance creativity, search for novel ideas, understand various perspectives, and make new discoveries and breakthrough innovations.[3] Simply being exposed to people who think differently than we do can change the way we think.

Studies have also found that when women and men work together in leadership roles, the organizations tend to be more open to diversity in hiring and promotions, employees are more satisfied with their jobs and have lower intentions to leave, workers have higher perceptions of fairness within the organizations, people

---

3. Phillips, "How Diversity Makes Us Smarter."

behave more ethically, and everyone is more likely to be engaged and involved.

One German study found that teams with women performed better on highly complex tasks because the different range of thinking patterns increased creativity.[4] Another study that focused on product development found that teams with both men and women produced more patents (licenses or approvals for inventions and new products).[5] Other researchers discovered that having more women in groups had been linked to effectiveness in solving difficult problems through what is called "higher collective intelligence." That means the group as a whole is much wiser than any individual person, teams with only men, or teams with only women.[6] Finally, researchers from the UK recently conducted a study with military participants and found that adding just one female's voice to an all-male team made a substantial difference.[7] They stated that teams with even one woman outperformed all-male teams in complex tasks. Of course, this only worked if the team members listened to the woman and acted on her suggestions. Unfortunately, that doesn't always happen.

It is important to note that having only one woman in a group of leaders is typically not the answer. Researchers through the years have concluded that having what is called "a critical mass" of three or more women on corporate boards makes a difference in terms of better leadership overall.[8] Other research says that the benefits mentioned above only emerge when women make up at least 30

---

4. Higgs, Plewnia, and Ploch, "Influence of Team Composition and Task Complexity on Team Performance."

5. Ashcraft and Breitzman, "Who Invents It? An Analysis of Women's Participation in Information Technology Patenting."

6. Woolley, Chabris, Pentland, Hashmi, and Malone, "Collective Intelligence: Number of Women in Group Linked to Effectiveness in Solving Difficult Problems."

7. Farh, Oh, Hollenbeck, Yu, Lee, and Kin, "Token Female Voice Enactment in Traditionally Male-Dominated Teams: Facilitating Conditions and Consequences for Performance."

8. Emelianova and Milhomem, "Women on Boards: 2019 Progress Report," 5.

percent of leadership team members.[9] Why? Because often if there are only one or two women in key discussions, they are interrupted, talked over, and discounted.[10] When this happens, the value that women can bring to decision making and problem solving substantially diminishes.

Here's an example of how this might play out in a ward or stake setting. Let's say that you are on a ward youth council or a member of a ward council, and the bishop asks for everyone to contribute their ideas on how to help a struggling individual or family in the ward. This could be a job loss, mental health challenges, a family member's health, and so on. The ward had already offered their typical services, such as delivered meals and the help of the employment specialist, but the situation has not improved. This is a complex problem, and the right solutions cannot typically be found on a checklist or in the General Handbook. If the discussion takes place with just young men and brethren, the solutions will be very different than if that discussion occurs with just young women and women. The solutions suggested from each of these groups will be "fine" or even "good," but will they be the best ideas and strategies? In most cases, probably not. When young men and young women or women and men—who all feel they can equally contribute— brainstorm together, the best ideas tend to emerge. If we truly want to help people around us, we need to problem-solve together.

For example, in terms of the previous example, a group made up of only brethren might come up with solutions focused on things like sending in the employment specialist, finding someone in the stake to help with car repairs for little or no cost, or working side by side with the father to do a major project on the house or yard. And these are all important efforts. An all-women's group might decide to take in meals, pick up the sister to do a session at the temple, or find sisters to watch her children so she can go to the doctor. Again, these are all important activities. However, for complex problems,

---

9. Madsen, "Why Do We Need More Women Leaders in Utah?"
10. Karpowitz and Mendelberg, *The Silent Sex: Gender, Deliberation, and Institutions.*

having both brothers and sisters brainstorming together can get to deeper solutions. For example, a multidimensional approach could emerge on how to provide deeper support for their teenage daughter who is in deep depression and needs support. This could include planning a youth activity where the daughter is asked to join a planning committee, finding a mentor or coach who has experience or expertise in mental health, creating a plan for both young men and women to reach out in ways that could demonstrate their love and appreciation for her, and more.

Of course, not every girl or woman is the same and not every boy or man is the same. We are all different, but the general findings from hundreds of studies are consistent. Overall, the varying viewpoints, ideas, and insights obtained from engaging both men and women in discussions can result in better problem solving and decision making.[11]

SPECIFIC CHARACTERISTICS AND ATTRIBUTES

In today's world, some people still believe that men are better leaders than women, but according to a number of studies in the last two decades, this is just not the case. Women tend to possess a significant number of characteristics and attributes that give them a leadership advantage in many ways. In fact, one study of 3,000 executives from nearly 150 countries found that employees rated women leaders higher than men.[12] Other researchers looked at data from 7,000 leaders and found that women outperformed men on most of the leadership competencies studied. Please note that I am *not* saying women are better leaders than men. I'm simply making the point that girls and women have every right to see themselves as effective and successful future leaders.

It is interesting to look at some of the research about the differences between women and men in terms of styles, attributes, skills,

---

11. Badal, "The Business Benefits of Gender Diversity."
12. Ibarra and Obodaru, "Women and the Vision Thing."

and characteristics. One large worldwide study[13] found that many of the female or feminine attributes are actually more valued in today's global and changing environments. For example, being collaborative, team-oriented, relationship-focused, empathetic, loyal, inclusive, flexible, intuitive, and passionate have become sought-after skills and qualities that most organizations now value. Other research states that women often have more skills in listening, provide more support to others in social situations, do not shy away from challenging issues, ask tough questions, want direct and detailed answers, and bring in the perspectives of others who many not be in the room.[14] In fact, women are often raised differently than men in that they tend to have a desire and ability to look for win-win instead of win-lose solutions. Girls and young women are raised to be more collaborative and connected than are boys and young men. And, for those areas that do not welcome these types of attributes—like many political settings—it is imperative that things change for the good of society.

Now, some of you might be like me: I was raised with six brothers and no sisters, so my leadership style is a bit of a mix between masculine and feminine characteristics. On the other hand, one of my brothers has a wonderful leadership style of listening, collaborating, caring, and more. Although I'm discussing generalities, I want to remind you that no two young women are alike, and there may be research findings that don't apply to you.

Did you know that women tend to be more holistic rather than linear thinkers and men the other way around? This means that we as girls and women often consider all the parts of a situation or project and how they might all be connected more thoroughly than a man might. Women might also see how one piece of the puzzle does or can impact or shift other parts of the situation or project. This relates to what is called right brain versus left brain work (more in later chapters).

---

13. Gerzema and D'Antonio, *The Athena Doctrine*.
14. McBaine, *Women at Church*, 102; Madsen, "Why Do We Need More Women Leaders in Utah?"

Did you also know that girls and women often have stronger abilities in reading nonverbal cues (for example, facial expressions, body language, tone of voice) and understanding what is happening in social interactions or situations? Many studies[15] have found that 55 percent of communication is body language, 38 percent is the tone of voice, and 7 percent is the actual words spoken. So, 93 percent of communication is nonverbal! That's a lot, and girls and women typically have stronger skills in observing and reading those cues. In part, this helps us be more nurturing, and we often care deeply about developing others around us. This makes women particularly powerful role models, mentors, and coaches.

Let me share an example of how nonverbal communication skills can be used in leadership. Let's say that you have an assignment to minister to a sister in your ward. Maybe you visited her in person and had planned to share a message with her. However, when you arrive you notice a stressed look on her face and some sadness in her eyes. Even though she has a forced smile on her face, you observe that the tone of her voice is not relaxed and welcoming. You glance around the room from the entrance where you are still standing and see that many things are just not as they typically are. Believe it or not, if you are paying attention, you can see all of this in ten to fifteen seconds. So, what do you do? Do you give her the prepared message? Do you quickly leave because you realize it is not a good time? Or do you give her a hug and ask her if you can help? It probably depends on the situation, right? Let's also say that you are a counselor in your Young Women class. Does that give you other options? What might your next steps be as a leader? If you lead on a sports team, in a high school student association, babysit a bunch of children, or sit on a youth city council, you can consider some additional scenarios in those settings as well.

---

15. Mehrabian, *Silent Messages: Implicit Communication of Emotions and Attitudes.*

DIFFERENT INTERESTS AND CHALLENGES

Did you know that women often ask different questions than men? Girls and women have different life experiences that bring with them unique insights, perspectives, concerns, and passions. The result is that women and men end up caring about different topics. Studies have shown that women often care more deeply about issues such as education, healthcare, and social programs to alleviate poverty, homelessness, and support victims of abuse. Women tend to put more energy toward efforts that directly impact children and families.

In fact, research has found that when women are on leadership teams of organizations, companies care more about their responsibility to the community and world,[16] are more responsive to the needs in society, and are more likely to engage in efforts to help and support in these areas. Multiple studies also found connections between greater numbers of women leaders and significantly higher levels of money donated to nonprofit organizations and community initiatives. Overall, women feel more compelled to be involved with efforts to help society—particularly families, children, the needy, and others who are underserved. These and other difficult issues and problems are much less likely to be ignored or brushed aside when women engage in leadership discussions.[17] These issues not only arise in government and politics, but also in decision-making roles within families, schools, nonprofits, church congregations, universities, and even businesses. Now, for those of you who think I'm recognizing women at the expense of men, this is not what I am doing at all. Men have many passions that are also important, but again the point is that when we serve and lead together, everyone benefits.[18]

To be honest, there are many challenges related to young women and women being valued and heard. It happens in many settings,

---

16. Catalyst, "Tool: Why Diversity Matters."
17. McBaine, *Women at Church*, 103.
18. Madsen, "Why Do We Need More Women Leaders in Utah?"

including in the Church. In fact, in his book *Counseling with Our Councils*, Elder M. Russell Ballard made the following statement: "It is a shortsighted priesthood leader who doesn't see the value in calling upon the sisters to share the understanding and inspiration they possess. . . . It is easy to understand why many sisters are frustrated when they sit in council with priesthood leaders and are not invited to make substantive contributions to the council."[19] He also mentioned that when most participants in leadership discussions are men—in any type of setting—women can feel at a disadvantage. Men tend to talk with other men and use different conversational styles from women who talk with other women. For example, men often interrupt and disagree with each other and emphasize differences of opinion. The research is clear that men and women often communicate differently in many ways, which can cause tension and misunderstandings.

Learning more about the similarities and differences between genders is very empowering. Instead of feeling frustrated, we can learn to appreciate, navigate, and educate each other. Wendy Ulrich, in her book *Live Up to Our Privileges: Women, Power, and Priesthood*, stated: "Most people are not conscious of these different norms. . . . But in mixed groups, men's style can leave women feeling dismissed, ignored, and threatened—and it is important for women to realize this is not usually intended or even conscious. At the same time, while men will fight for airtime, women will tend to defer and stop talking, unintentionally setting themselves up to feel ignored and to blame men for the problem."[20] In fact, one set of researchers has repeatedly found that women talk significantly less in groups of mostly men, and for the most part only equalize in terms of talking and feeling valued when there are more women in the group than men.[21]

---

19. Ballard, *Counseling with Our Councils*, 58, 62.
20. Ulrich, *Live Up to Our Privileges: Women, Power, and Priesthood*, 141.
21. Karpowitz and Mendelberg, *The Silent Sex: Gender, Deliberation, and Institutions*.

CONCLUSION

This chapter has focused on research surrounding the importance of gender balanced leadership, why decision making and problem solving are better when men and women lead together, the specific characteristics and attributes women have that make them effective leaders, and some of the different interests and challenges women have compared to men. For those of you who really appreciated this content, you'll enjoy the additional details I've sprinkled throughout the rest of the book. And for the rest of you who are eager to get specifics on how to become a leader, we are almost there!

I previously brought up the point that sometimes people think these types of conversations lift girls and women at the expense of boys and men. I've discovered that this is more common when people in our society have what is called a "fixed mindset" (see later chapter for details) or a "zero-sum mentality"—that if we lift women, we will take away from men. Let's discard this widely held myth. We can lift and support girls and women, while also lifting and supporting boys, men, families, and society (including people of all races, backgrounds, and life experiences).

I love what Sheri L. Dew, former counselor in the Relief Society General Presidency, said in a talk she gave in general conference many years ago: "No marriage or family, no ward or stake is likely to reach its full potential until husbands and wives, mothers and fathers, men and women work together in unity of purpose, respecting and relying upon each other's strengths."[22]

When more women and men work productively together—particularly on complex problems—in a variety of settings, situations, and circumstances, better decisions will be made. And this world needs better dialogue, discussions, and decisions!

---

22. Dew, "It Is Not Good for Man or Woman to Be Alone," 13.

CHAPTER 4

Leadership Opportunities Around Us

"What you do makes a difference, and you have to decide what kind of difference you want to make."

—JANE GOODALL

As teen and you adult women in The Church of Jesus Christ of Latter-day Saints, each of you needs to be prepared to lead in a variety of situations, circumstances, and settings. Through the years, a few college students have told me that they don't need to learn certain material or develop certain competencies—like critical thinking, writing, public speaking, teamwork, leadership, or business ethics—because they will "never use it." By now, you can probably guess how I might have responded. I would point out that they have no idea what life will bring them and what unexpected opportunities might present themselves. Basically, if you are not prepared, you will not be asked. If you are not asked, then you cannot say "yes." The point of this whole book is that you need to be prepared for a future only God can see for you. This means that you will need to be prepared for anything you may need to or be asked to do, and for opportunities which you may feel prompted to take on.

This happens to me all the time. Because I have prepared to lead, I get asked to be involved in many groups that drive critical efforts

37

and make meaningful decisions. I am proactive as well. When I see important strategic opportunities that I know I can positively influence, I make it known that I'm willing to be involved. Because of my preparation, I know that my knowledge, abilities, voice, and values are important to help guide decisions that could impact thousands of lives. Being prepared to lead is the key.

This chapter will focus on the types of leadership opportunities that may arise if you are prepared. Leadership can happen in any setting, but this chapter will focus on the following three core areas: family, church, and community. Of course, I won't be able to highlight all of the settings or circumstances you may have opportunities in which to lead, but my hope is that this chapter will help expand your current mindset on the potential leadership situations that could arise. As former Young Women General President Elaine S. Dalton declared: "As daughters of God, you were born to lead."[1]

FAMILY

First, Church leaders teach us that men and women should be co-leaders in their homes. According to professors Valerie Hudson and Richard B. Miller, in their 2013 article in the *Ensign*, "The restored gospel of Jesus Christ proclaims the doctrine of equal partnership between men and women, here and in the eternities." They then explain that equality is often mistaken to mean that "if two things are equal, they must be identical to each other."[2] We are taught that men and women should walk side by side with neither one before nor behind the other. Drs. Hudson and Miller also stated that "in the plan of happiness, man and woman play equally powerful and equally important roles. For the plan to work, each must hearken to the other. Before God, they stand as equals."[3] If there is a husband and wife in the home, leadership strategies and decisions should be made together. And if, for any reason, a

---

1. Dalton, "Now is the Time to Arise and Shine!" 123.
2. Hudson and Miller, "Equal Partnerships in Marriage," 19.
3. Ibid., 21.

woman does not have a partner, she will be the sole leader in the home. No matter a woman's circumstance, alone or with her husband, she is a leader in the family.

Many people do not acknowledge that mothering—which often comes with giving birth and raising your own children but can also occur by influencing children and youth around you—is a form of leadership. In fact, I've had women tell me they have never held a leadership role in their lives. Yet, they may have four teenagers in their home—and leading teenagers in the home is one of most demanding types of leadership I've ever seen. This is true for children of all ages. Now, take a minute and reflect on the definition of leadership I provided in the second chapter in connection to mothering. Leading children is a *process* of *influencing* a *group of people* toward a *goal*. While my husband and I raised four children, we always had a variety of goals in our home from keeping the house clean, to family unity and living righteously, to serving others, to teaching our children to use their voices to defend the gospel.

Even as a teenager or young adult, you can lead in your homes in various situations and settings right now. For example, when you oversee your younger siblings—I'm talking about babysitting, but I was trying to make it sound fancier—you are leading. When you encourage other family members to complete *Come, Follow Me* for the week, you are leading. You can practice leading all the time in your own homes. And, as Gordon T. Smith, author of *Courage and Calling: Embracing Your God-given Potential* stated, "Real power comes in the capacity to bless."[4]

When Sharon Eubank, First Counselor in the General Presidency of the Relief Society, came to speak for an event I hosted in 2020, she stated: "I never want to discount the power of individuals themselves to create change at that family level. With the dynamics of what's going on in our own families. . . . I think that changes the

---

4. Smith, *Courage and Calling: Embracing Your God-given Potential*, 71.

world."[5] Creating change is leading. Leadership in our own homes is the most important kind of leadership there is.

CHURCH

Another reason girls and women should prepare to lead is to be ready for a lifetime of leadership callings within wards and stakes. In his general conference talk entitled "Covenant Women in Partnership with God," President Henry B. Eyring counseled, "In the same way that you prepare to minister, you can and must prepare for your call to be a leader for the Lord when it comes. It will require faith in Jesus Christ, rooted in your deep love of the scriptures, to lead people and to teach His word without fear."[6]

Callings as young women could include serving in class presidencies, teaching lessons, planning and running meetings and activities, setting a good example by listening and participating in lessons and events, taking on responsibilities at girl's camp, or other special assignment given by the bishopric or Young Women presidencies and advisors. There are a few opportunities to lead in stake positions as well. A young woman in a Young Single Adult (YSA) ward or stake could also identify various opportunities to lead. Bonnie L. Oscarson, former Young Women General President, urged you to see yourselves as "essential participants in the priesthood-directed work of salvation and not just as onlookers and supporters. You hold callings and are set apart by those holding priesthood keys to function as leaders with power and authority in this work."[7] Using your voice in councils within the Church is becoming more important than ever before. Don't just sit and listen. Use your voice.

Neylan McBaine wrote in her book *Women at Church*, "When women claim their voices by attending meetings, speaking up in meetings, embracing opportunities to speak about doctrine, and

---

5. Madsen, "Honor International Women's Day by Becoming Empowered as Global Citizens."
6. Eyring, "Covenant Women in Partnership with God," 72.
7. Oscarson, "Rise Up in Strength, Sisters in Zion," 14.

being visible symbols of female participation, they pave the way for their daughters and granddaughters to feel more integrated into the Church's administrative and ecclesiastical dialogues and thus less likely to feel silenced or undervalued." This is a powerful form of leadership as well.[8]

Sheri L. Dew believes that women get more leadership opportunities in the Church than in any other religion around the world. In her book *Women and the Priesthood*, she noted many ways that we as sisters lead. We pray, preach, expound, direct, teach, preside, serve, and oversee. Women also serve on councils and officiate in priesthood ordinances for women in the temple.[9] And Relief Society general board member Wendy Ulrich noted, "The teachings of modern apostles and prophets clarify that women serve in the Church today with both priesthood authority and priesthood power."[10]

Serving a full-time mission as a young adult is another way you can both be a leader in the Church and prepare for future leadership roles. I led a research team a few years ago that studied how missions prepared young adult women to lead, and the results were profound. These returned sister missionaries had gained or strengthened hundreds of leadership competencies related to a variety of interpersonal and relationships skills, professional and practical abilities, courage and confidence, personal growth and maturity, and managing challenges.[11]

We just scratched the surface, but hopefully this gives you some ideas about what women's leadership in the Church might look like. But it is also important to remember that you can lead in ways you feel *called to* within Church settings, even if it is not a formal calling. For example, I don't have a formal calling to write this book, but I feel *called* by God to write it. I get asked to speak at firesides, but that is not a formal calling either. Regardless of how you serve,

---

8. McBaine, *Women at Church*, 114.
9. Dew, *Women and the Priesthood*, 86.
10. Ulrich, *Live Up to Our Privileges*, 1.
11. Madsen, Scribner, Fox-Kirk, and Lafkas, "The Leadership Development Gained by Women Serving Full-time Missions."

President Russell M. Nelson explained that "whether by exhortation or conversation, we need your voice teaching the doctrine of Christ. We need your input in family, ward, and stake councils. Your participation is essential and never ornamental!"[12]

COMMUNITY

Women and men have many opportunities to lead in their communities, including 1) running for and serving in political elected office, 2) serving on committees, boards, and commissions, 3) leading efforts to change and improve society, 4) obtaining influential roles with educational institutions, 5) volunteering for leadership roles in programs or projects led by government, nongovernmental organizations (nonprofit), and other types of entities, and 6) embracing leadership roles within your places of work.

First, in a 2018 session of general conference, President M. Russell Ballard of the Quorum of the Twelve Apostles remarked: "Church members—both men and women—should not hesitate, if they desire, to run for public office at any level of government wherever they live. Our voices are essential today and important in our schools, our cities, and our countries. Where democracy exists, it is our duty as members to vote for honorable men and women who are willing to serve."[13] President Ballard used the phrase "if they desire," which can be problematic, because boys and men are brought up much more often to want to serve in these ways. To have more young women "desire" to run, we need to help more girls and women—like you—see the benefits of serving in these positions and why it is worth taking the journey. Having women and men serve side by side as elected officials benefits everyone (see chapter 3). More than ever before, we need more women to run for and serve in elected positions at all levels (school board, municipal, county, state, region, and country). Volunteering to assist good, honest, and ethical women and men as they run for these positions is another way to serve and lead as well.

---

12. Nelson, "Spiritual Treasures," 79.
13. Ballard, "Precious Gifts from God," 10.

Second, in addition to elected positions of influence, women can also serve in appointed municipal, county, and state committees, boards, and commissions. Sister Sharon Eubank stated that "the women of this Church have unlimited potential to change society."[14] And, Carole M. Stephens, former First Counselor in the Relief Society General Presidency, stated: "As daughters of God and disciples of Jesus Christ, we then 'act according to those sympathies which God has planted' in our hearts. Our sphere of influence isn't limited to our own family members."[15] We cannot just sit back and wait to be appointed. Appointments come when women step forward to use their voices and serve as volunteers in areas in which they are passionate and educated.

Third, women can use their voices to address and resolve many societal challenges. For example, Sarah M. Kimball, a pioneer and early member of the Relief Society general board, "advocated for the equality and rights of women, including promoting women's suffrage in the 1870s and 1880s in Utah," leading to Utah women obtaining the right to vote.[16] She participated in meetings of the National Council of Women and helped coordinate efforts of various women's rights organizations. Challenges like domestic and sexual assault, maternal mental health, air quality, ethical leadership, voter participation levels, parental leave policies, public school curriculum, gender wage gap, teacher pay, and a myriad of other topics need support from women who are educated on the issues and civil and respectful in their demeanors. In the beginning days of the restored Church, General Relief Society President Eliza R. Snow noted that President Brigham Young had "turned the key to a wide and extensive sphere of action and usefulness" for women.[17]

Fourth, there are always ample ways to get involved and lead in educational institutions, like schools, colleges and universities, and adult learning and job preparation programs. This can include leading

---

14. Eubank, "By Union of Feeling We Obtain Power with God," 54.
15. Stephens, "The Family Is of God," 12.
16. Reeder and Holbrooke, *At the Pulpit*, 90.
17. *Daughters in My Kingdom*, 39.

a parent's association, starting a group to discuss improving students' mental health resources, serving as an advisor or ambassador to an academic program, organizing a mentoring program for a school within the local college, or speaking for a job preparation program. You can have a righteous influence in any of these initiatives. In some countries, the available opportunities may be more limiting or look quite different, but there are opportunities to lead wherever you live.

Fifth, women can volunteer for leadership roles in programs or projects led by government, nongovernmental organizations (nonprofit), and other types of entities. In addition to time, we can donate money to help as well. I know many Latter-day Saint women who have created new humanitarian initiatives, built cultural institutions, advanced programs, and started their own nonprofit organizations. Nothing feels better than contributing time, money, or support in other ways that truly make a difference. President M. Russell Ballard stated that "every sister in this Church who has made covenants with the Lord has a divine mandate to help save souls, to lead the women of the world, to strengthen the homes of Zion, and to build the kingdom of God."[18] Leading in these ways can help address this important call.

And, finally, we can also prepare to lead in our workplaces, wherever those may be. Paid work can be found in all the types of efforts and organizations I have just discussed (such as government, political, nonprofit, schools, and universities) as well as in for-profit companies. Strong women of influence within companies can improve the lives of their employees, clients, and customers in ways that can impact thousands. The presence of women in key leadership roles can improve fairness and equality in decision-making, increase the support that is given in terms of flexibility and family-friendly policies, and ensure that the workplace cultures are respectful to all employees no matter their gender, race, ethnicity, ability, sexual orientation, and other characteristics. Helping all employees feel like they belong is often a focus of women leaders in any type of organization.

---

18. Ibid., 25.

CONCLUSION

You don't need to wait for someone to tell you what you should do with your gifts, talents, and power. According to General Relief Society President Jean B. Bingham, "We have the ability to receive revelation for ourselves. We shouldn't wait to be acted upon; we need to have the courage to act on the revelation that we receive."[19] As Elaine S. Dalton, in her book *No Ordinary Women*, proclaimed, "Never before has there been a time of such limitless opportunity to connect with others in the world—to serve, to testify, and to make a difference."[20] We have been prepared and positioned on this earth to do just that.

Converted, covenant-keeping women who are members of The Church of Jesus Christ of Latter-day Saints are needed as leaders everywhere. This is one of the reasons it is so important for you, as teen and young adult women, to prepare now to influence and lead. I believe that the need for honest, ethical, and courageous leaders will substantially increase in coming years in all settings. In 1974, the General Relief Society President of the Church, Belle S. Spafford, remarked: "Today a woman's world is as broad as the universe. There's scarcely an area of human endeavor that a woman cannot enter if she has the will and preparation to do so."[21] When you combine the forces of millions of sisters around the world, "there is no limit to what they can achieve."[22] I support and encourage all to answer the call that Sharon Eubank, the director of Latter-day Saint Charities, offered to sisters everywhere: "Be part of a collective force that changes the world for good."[23]

---

19. Bingham, "Women and Covenant Power," 24.
20. Dalton, *No Ordinary Women*, 64.
21. "Reaching Every Facet of a Woman's Life: A Conversation with Belle S. Spafford, Relief Society General President," para. 8.
22. "Sister Bingham United Nations Transcript: Focus on Faith Briefing Remarks," para. 4.
23. Eubank, "By Union of Feeling We Obtain Power with God," 57.

PART II

Preparing to Lead

CHAPTER 5

Confidence

"No one can make me feel inferior without my consent."

—ELEANOR ROOSEVELT

To prepare for "a future greater than anything you can imagine" and to become that "person of glory and light"[1] you have the potential to become, God needs you to prepare to lead. Part II of this book helps you do this by teaching you how to strengthen your confidence (chapter 5), discover your gifts, talents, and strengths (chapter 6), boost your growth mindset (chapter 7), pursue learning and education (chapter 8), explore your purpose and callings (chapter 9), and embrace your leadership identity (chapter 10). More than ever before in the history of this world, I believe that our Heavenly Parents need sisters to be covenant-keeping, committed, and *confident*!

In his 2015 general conference talked titled "A Plea to My Sisters,"[2] President Russell M. Nelson highlighted at least fourteen things that Latter-day Saint sisters need to become and do. He said the Lord needs women who make important things happen by their faith, are courageous defenders of virtue and families,

---

1. Uchtdorf, "Living the Gospel Joyful," 121.
2. Nelson, "A Plea to My Sisters," 95–96.

righteously shepherd God's children along the covenant path, know how to receive personal revelation, understand the power and peace that can come from our temple covenants, know how to "call upon the powers of heaven to protect and strengthen children and families," teach fearlessly, "have a bedrock understanding of the doctrine of Christ," teach those doctrines to others, can detect deception, know how to access the power of God, can express their beliefs with confidence and charity, and have courage and vision. President Nelson also emphasized the importance of developing virtue, light, love, knowledge, courage, character, faith, righteousness, strength, conversion, conviction, an ability to lead, wisdom, and confident voices. Since each of these takes confidence in one way or another, this will be the focus of the first chapter in part II on "Preparing to Lead."

Although you can have "confidence" in Heavenly Father and in other people, this chapter will focus on confidence in yourself. I will discuss what confidence is, the gender differences in confidence, a few behaviors that limit our confidence, and ways you can strengthen your confidence moving forward.

DEFINITIONS

Confidence is different from optimism, self-awareness, self-compassion, self-concept, self-efficacy, self-esteem, and self-worth. Of course, they are all related to each other in various ways, but confidence is distinct. We often use some of these words interchangeably, but I want to help you understand the differences.

Confidence is not just thinking you are a wonderful person. It is a feeling, belief, or attitude of trusting or being certain in your own abilities, skills, qualities, and judgment. In fact, you can only strengthen your confidence through action—doing things, practicing, and getting better. Confidence is the "stuff that turns thoughts into action."[3] It can even take the judgments that we have about ourselves—self-worth and self-esteem—and

---

3. Kay and Shipman, *The Confidence Code*, 50.

transform them into action. It is an assurance or trust that we can do or become something because we have practiced and learned. For example, if you play the piano and have practiced a song, you have confidence that you can play it. And the more you practice, the more confident you become. The confidence you get from mastering one task is contagious and can help you master other things as well.

As I said, each of these terms is closely aligned and interrelated, but confidence has some unique elements. Take a minute to read the definitions in Table 5.1 (Related Terms and Definitions), as these will be mentioned in this chapter and throughout the book.

Table 5.1: Related Terms and Definitions[4]

Confidence	A feeling, belief, or attitude of trusting or being certain in your own abilities, skills, qualities, and judgment. Includes assurance, courage, and trust to believe in yourself and then act on those beliefs.
Optimism	A belief, feeling, and hope that good things will happen in the future. A confidence and hopefulness for a positive or successful outcome. Emphasizes the good parts of a situation or circumstance.
Self-awareness	A realization (knowledge and awareness) of yourself as an individual and personality. Includes the extent to which your self-knowledge is defined, consistent, and currently applicable to your attitudes and dispositions.
Self-compassion	Extending compassion to yourself, particularly in circumstances where you believe you have failed, suffered, or are inadequate. Involves being kind to yourself and understanding you are only human.

---

4.   Definitions gathered and adapted from several different dictionaries.

Self-concept	The idea or mental image you have of yourself, including your strengths, weaknesses, and status. Includes the beliefs you have about yourself, your attributes, who you are, and how you are different from others.
Self-efficacy	A belief or personal judgment that you can be successful at doing or coping with a specific task, assignment, or circumstance you will face. The confidence you have in your own ability to do something specific.
Self-esteem	A feeling of having respect for, satisfaction with, or a favorable impression of yourself and your abilities. It is self-evaluation of your own worth, and it encompasses the beliefs you have about yourself.
Self-worth	A sense of your own value and worth as a human being, a feeling that you are a good person who deserves to be treated with respect, and the value you give to your life and what you have done.

If you have low levels of self-esteem, self-worth, and self-efficacy, you will struggle strengthening your confidence. You need to believe you have worth and can be valued and respected to have confidence in yourself. The more you are self-aware and understand your self-concept, the more you will be able to strategically work on your confidence. In addition, optimism is critical to confidence because you must have hope to even attempt to improve. And self-compassion, believe it or not, is also foundational to confidence. Again, you must do and act to strengthen your confidence. The more you *act*, the more likely you will succeed, but it is also likely that you will fail more often. Self-compassion helps you pick yourself up and dust yourself off when you make mistakes. Strangely enough, learning to be okay with failure is one of the foundational strategies to strengthen your confidence. Imagine that piano piece again. As you play you may stumble over parts or hit the wrong key. But all that is part of practice, part of learning where you need to slow down and focus. The mistakes, over time, help you improve and play more surely.

So why do we need confidence? Confidence is an essential life ingredient, and we need it every hour and every day of our lives to do pretty much anything.[5] In fact, confidence is linked to almost every element involved in a happy and fulfilling life. Without it, we cannot succeed as we could, and we can't even envision the opportunities we might have to contribute in meaningful ways.[6] Confidence is essential in becoming that "person of glory and light" we have the potential to become.[7]

GENDER DIFFERENCES

Understanding gender differences can be helpful as you work on strengthening your own confidence. Research tells us that women are less self-assured than men, have more self-doubt, get more anxious when leaving their comfort zones, overthink and don't let go of defeats or mistakes as quickly, have hurt feelings longer, judge themselves harder, take longer to get started again after failure, don't use failure to learn as well, and beat themselves up more often than men.[8] Of course men doubt themselves sometimes as well, but they don't let that hold them back as women often do.[9] But it's not your fault! This confidence gap happens for many reasons that I'll discuss.

Researchers have found that this is generally true across cultures, incomes, ages, professions, and generations. Nearly all girls and women struggle with confidence in certain areas at one time or another. Researchers have found that confidence is made up of three key attributes: 1) genetics, 2) our upbringing and socialization, and 3) one's own choice. I will provide a quick overview of these areas and invite you to study and learn more about each.

---

5. Kay and Shipman, *The Confidence Code*, xv.
6. Ibid., 24.
7. Uchtdorf, "Living the Gospel Joyful," 123.
8. Kay and Shipman, *The Confidence Code*, 111.
9. Kay and Shipman, "The Confidence Gap," para. 25.

First, there are differences between boys and girls in terms of genetics—no surprise there. Although male and female brains are much more alike than different, there are enough differences that researchers have concluded girls and women have unique thinking and behavior patterns that impact confidence.[10] These include differences in brain structure, hormones, neurotransmitters, and more. For example, women have more estrogen and men more testosterone, and those levels influence us in profound ways. Estrogen influences increased social and observational skills, including bonding and connection, and it discourages conflict and risk taking. If you want more detail about the differences in genetics between men and women, particularly on how this influences confidence, I suggest that you read *The Confidence Code: The Science and Art of Self-Assurance—What Women Should Know* by Katty Kay and Claire Shipman. In fact, it is a great book if you want to learn more about confidence in general.

Second, the way girls and boys are raised—our upbringing—impacts the confidence levels of young women and young men. For example, early influencers (such as parents, siblings, extended family, teachers in elementary school and church) socialize girls to avoid taking risks because they step in to help them more often. In addition, girls are socialized to seek out praise more than boys, which impacts their confidence throughout their lives. Finally, boys are more likely to be raised knowing they can choose nearly any college major in anything they would like to, while young women often feel they can only major in certain fields. Of course, there are always exceptions, but we should be aware of these past and current influences in our lives and how they impact confidence.

Even the types of service and activities that young women and young men do in the Church are different. Think about the differences between annual camps for young men and young women. In school and community programs, more boys are enrolled early on in sports and other types of competitive activities, like speech and

---

10. Ibid., para. 37.

debate, and are encouraged more strongly to continue these activities throughout high school. Everything we experience as we are growing up can impact our confidence.

Finally, although a big chunk of our initial confidence can be attributed to genetics and socialization, a great deal of building confidence only happens as we change our assumptions and perspectives. Confidence can be a choice, and therefore, a lack of confidence can also be a choice. This is important, because seeing confidence as a matter of choice removes it from the passive arenas of genetics and upbringing. Even though our thoughts create neural pathways in our brains, we can change our brains in ways that will affect our thoughts and behaviors. We can reflect on the choices we make and set goals to make decisions that will increase our confidence, sphere of influence, and leadership abilities and aptitudes. Although this is a simple concept, it doesn't mean it's easy to do. Changing our perspective can feel scary and daunting. We may have to recommit to doing this over and over again. But it is possible.

LIMITING BEHAVIORS

Based on genetics, socialization, and the choices we make, many behaviors limit our confidence, either by thwarting our initial development of confidence or by negatively impacting it along the way. Even though there are hundreds of these limiting behaviors, I'll discuss three that are particularly problematic: rumination, perfectionism, and avoiding risks.

Rumination

Women ruminate more than men. This means that we get into obsessive thinking patterns about something (an idea, situation, or choice) that can go on and on. We spend far too much time overthinking and dwelling on problems rather than solutions. We focus too much on why we did certain things, how poorly we did them, what everyone else was thinking about it, and how we look. Rumination can freeze decision making and action, and it drains confidence.[11] Rumination often accompanies feelings that we are not good enough and tendencies to be hard on ourselves. I've always appreciated a statement from Eleanor Roosevelt, former First Lady of the United States: "You wouldn't worry so much about what others think of you if you realized how seldom they do."[12] Rumination stops you from doing and acting, the very keys to confidence.

Perfectionism

Women are also much more perfectionistic than are men. In fact, there is interesting research specifically on women in the Church, toxic perfectionism, and depression.[13] They are connected. Because perfectionism stops you from doing and acting, it does not allow confidence to growth and develop. It keeps us from taking risks, making decisions, and moving forward. As the authors of the *The Confidence Code* stated, "Study after study confirms that it is largely a female issue, one that extends through women's entire lives. We don't answer questions until we are totally sure of the answer, we don't submit a report until we've edited it ad nauseam, and we don't sign up for that triathlon unless we know we are faster and fitter than is required. We watch our male colleagues take risks, while we hold back until we're sure we are perfectly ready and perfectly qualified. We fixate on our performance at home, at school, at work, at yoga class, even on vacation. . . . The irony is that striving to be perfect actually keeps us from getting much of anything done."[14] Overall, the more perfectionistic we are, the less confidence we can gain. And, if we are worried about being perfect then we don't act. And remember, action is the way we strengthen our confidence.

Avoiding Risks

Women generally take far fewer risks than do men for many reasons, and they all revolve around genetics and socialization. For

---

11. Kay and Shipman, *The Confidence Code*, 104.
12. Roosevelt, "10 Inspiring Quotes by Eleanor Roosevelt."
13. Benson & Jackson, "Nobody's Perfect: A Look at Toxic Perfectionism and Depression."
14. Kay and Shipman, "The Confidence Gap," para. 34.

example, the average man has ten times more testosterone than the average woman, which is the hormone associated with taking more risks. On top of this, most girls are raised to take fewer risks and are not given the opportunities needed to get used to taking them. In fact, one group of researchers studied how mothers and fathers socialized their daughters and sons differently. In this study, fathers of sons encouraged boys to take risks, but fathers of daughters were more likely to watch, protect, and help their daughters avoid risks. Interestingly, mothers of daughters and sons treated both pretty much the same.[15] Another reason girls and women avoid risks is that they worry more than boys and men, which can undermine confidence. But there is good news: the more girls succeed, the more they are willing to try new things and subsequently to develop a sense of their own capabilities. Remember that a risk can be as small as just talking to someone new at school. As girls and women, we often want to stay in our comfort zones because we don't like to fail.

An example of how these three areas can negatively impact a young woman might go as follows: As you prepare for a piano recital, you mess up on one part of a difficult piece. That night you ruminate on your mistake, going over and over it until that's all you remember about your playing. You convince yourself that if you can't perform it flawlessly, and you don't want to play it at all. You decide to tell your teacher that you want to play a simpler song for the recital because you don't want to risk messing up on the more advanced piece. This thinking has undermined your ability to grow your confidence.

Of course, there are so many other limiting behaviors that I could have discussed from giving in to imposter syndrome ("the persistent inability to believe that one's success is deserved or has been legitimately achieved as a result of one's own efforts or skills"),[16] putting yourself in situations where you are treated as "less than,"

---

15. Hagan & Kuebli, "Mothers' and Fathers' Socialization of Preschoolers' Physical Risk Taking."
16. *Lexico Dictionary*, s.v., "Imposter Syndrome."

to thinking patterns of feeling undeserving of love, and to eating disorders and other mental health challenges. Unfortunately, if you don't have the tools to turn things around, each of these situations can result in confidence challenges at varying levels and in a variety of ways. But there is hope!

STRATEGIES

You can use many strategies to strengthen your confidence, including the ones that will be discussed in upcoming chapters. But to start, here are eight research-based strategies that can help you and your friends continue along your path of confidence building:[17]

1. **Break Rumination Cycles:** Because rumination is a habit, you will need to break these patterns, form new habits, and create more productive responses. Learn more about how your mind works so you don't spend time overthinking your choices, responses, and actions.

2. **Reduce Pointless Perfection:** Identify which areas of your life you feel you need to be perfect in, including areas where you don't even want to try or are more afraid of failure. Being aware will help. Teach yourself to feel satisfied when you have done your best, regardless of how you compare to others.

3. **Decrease Reliance on Praise:** Since girls are socialized more often than boys to rely on the praise of others, shifting this behavior will take deep internal work. Begin by reflecting on when, how, and why you seek external praise. Shift from the need for external praise to finding internal fulfillment and satisfaction.

4. **Take Chances:** Take more risks. This can include talking to someone new, giving a talk in church, accepting a calling that makes you uncomfortable, asking a friend at school to

---

17. Kay and Shipman, "The Confidence Gap."

come to church, or any number of things. Push yourself out of your comfort zone and try new and difficult things.

5. **Get Comfortable Failing More Often:** Taking risks may mean that you fail more often. If you aren't failing from time to time, you probably aren't learning and growing as much as you could. "Fail fast" is a term that is often used, which means that you figure out more quickly what works and what doesn't. Reframe failure as a chance to learn.

6. **Embrace Challenges:** Embracing challenges is the best way you can develop leadership. In fact, one study found that 70 percent of leadership development is gained from challenging assignments.[18] Look for a hard task, take it on, and focus on the learning it provides.

7. **Become Intentionally Uncomfortable:** Research shows that if you are comfortable, then you are most likely not learning. Become comfortable with being uncomfortable by pushing yourself over and over to do things that are outside your comfort zone. The more you do this, the more confidence you will gain.

8. **Practice Self-Compassion:** Having self-compassion means that you treat yourself like you would treat a friend or someone else that you love and respect. Give yourself a break, because you are only human. Forgive yourself. You cannot be perfect, so practice saying, "I did the best I can, and I'm moving on!" Criticizing yourself doesn't help.

Eleanor Roosevelt once wrote: "You gain strength, courage, and confidence by every experience in which you really stop to look fear in the face. You are able to say to yourself, 'I lived through this horror. I can take the next thing that comes along.' You must do the thing you think you cannot." Maybe you don't live through "horror" and maybe you do, but I think her point is important: Doing hard things helps us grow, which then strengthens our confidence. If we stay

---

18. Clerkin and Wilson, "Gender Differences in Developmental Experiences."

clear of challenging situations or opportunities, we cannot prepare ourselves to lead in the ways the Lord needs us to lead in future years. As was once proclaimed: "There are always two choices. Two paths to take. One is easy. And its only reward is that it's easy."[19]

CONCLUSION

Bonnie L. Oscarson, former Young Women General President, said, "Your teenage years can be busy and often challenging. We have noticed that many more of you are struggling with issues of self-worth, anxiety, high levels of stress, and perhaps even depression. Turning your thoughts outward, instead of dwelling on your own problems, may not resolve all of these issues, but service can often lighten your burdens and make your challenges seem less hard. One of the best ways to increase feelings of self-worth is to show, through our concern and service to others, that we have much of worth to contribute."[20] I believe that these things can also strengthen our confidence.

I love reading the writings of Eliza R. Snow, one of my pioneer heroes from Church history. I'm sure she had many struggles throughout her life, and I expect at times she felt that she wasn't good enough or gifted enough or even worthy enough. We all do. Yet, she wrote the following inspiring passage: "I will go forward. . . . I will smile at the rage of the tempest, and ride fearlessly and triumphantly across the boisterous ocean of circumstance. . . . And the 'testimony of Jesus' will light up a lamp that will guide my vision through the portals of immortality, and communicate to my understanding the glories of the Celestial kingdom."[21] Talk about confidence! Ultimately, the courage to take action, which is essential to building confidence, will grow as we strive to love the Lord, love ourselves, and love and serve others.

---

19. Anonymous.
20. Oscarson, "Young Women in the Work," 38.
21. Snow, *Poems, Religious, Historical, and Political, Vol. 1*, 148–149.

CHAPTER 6

Gifts, Talents, and Strengths

"Know that your Heavenly Father will provide all that you need to become 'extra'-ordinary as a daughter of God. The wonder of His heavenly economy is that every single one of us can be spectacular because of our unique bundle of talents and abilities. Unlike the world, in His Kingdom there is no winner's platform that only has room for one or two. Each of His daughters has been taught and prepared and gifted premortally with marvelous potential to become a queen in the celestial kingdom."

—PRESIDENT JEAN B. BINGHAM[1]

I am continually surprised by the thousands of amazing and gifted teen and young adult women I've met through the years who have no clue how remarkable they are. Yet, everyone born on this earth is unlike anyone else. Each of you is a unique, gifted, extraordinary young woman who is distinct from every individual throughout the

---

1.   Bingham, "How Vast is Our Purpose," para. 3.

history of the world. In fact, historians believe that more than 100 billion people have lived on the earth. That is a lot of people!

Yet, I have found that most girls and women struggle to see their *distinct uniqueness* and how they can use their combination of strengths in ways no one else can. We must remember that our Heavenly Parents made each of us very different on purpose, to serve and impact in distinct ways. Because of this, I truly believe that God needs each of us to do our part to strengthen His Church and to bring more souls to Him.

Former Young Women President Elaine S. Dalton once wrote, "You and I have been prepared and reserved to be here on the earth now, uniquely positioned in time and place to make a difference, to contribute and lead in such a way that our righteous influence will change the world. I know it is possible. Our opportunities for leadership and service are not only in our families, our neighborhoods, our communities, and in the Church, but in the world as well. Each of us came to the earth with gifts and talents to help us accomplish our part."[2]

To effectively prepare to influence and lead, you will need to become more aware of your gifts, talents, and strengths. This chapter will begin by defining and providing examples of each of these terms. I then offer some background on how each of us is unique, a discussion on the distractors that keep us from embracing our talents, and strategies on how to better recognize our gifts, talents, and strengths.

DEFINITIONS

When I speak about this topic, I generally use the three words *gifts*, *talents*, and *strengths*. I do this because I not only want to cover my bases, but I also believe that, even though there is overlap, each has its own distinct meaning.

First, a *gift* in this context is something that is given to us either from God or from someone responsible for us, like our parents. Gifts are special capacities or opportunities that are bestowed upon us without being earned or without any particular effort on

---

2.   Dalton, *No Ordinary Women*, 7.

our part. These can include talents (see below), tender mercies and specific blessings, the Atonement and plan of happiness, or even circumstances in which we find ourselves. For example, a gift could include having loving and supportive parents (many people do not), being able to grow up in a safe and enriching environment, involvement in extracurricular activities, or even being put into difficult circumstances that provide opportunities to learn and grow. Honestly, I think one of our biggest challenges is identifying and recognizing the gifts we have been given. If we are not consciously aware, we won't effectively harness the benefits these gifts can provide to propel us forward in our preparation to lead.

Second, *talents* are natural abilities that are innate within us. We are each born with certain capabilities that are natural ways of thinking, feeling, or behaving that can be developed into strengths. Do you remember the parable of the talents (see Matthew 25)? A man gave five talents to one servant, two to another, and one to the last. Then Jesus Christ taught that we should develop and use our talents, not hide or ignore them because we don't feel like we have enough. This is true. Now, talents can include skills such as playing the piano, speaking in public, being a top athlete, or exceling as a lead in a school play. However, talents can also include attributes such as kindness, courage, responsibility, dependability, positivity, boldness, inclusivity, empathy, compassion, attentiveness, assertiveness, and resilience. The problem is never that we don't have enough talents. The trouble is when we don't fully develop the ones God has given us.

Finally, Gallup[3]—creator of the *StrengthsFinder* and *Clifton Strengths for Students* assessments—has taught that a true **strength** must start with natural talents that then must be developed through the years. Turning *talents* into strengths takes learning, practice, and repetition. Talents only become strengths if we develop them by gaining related knowledge and skills. Knowledge comes from learning, and skills can only be built through practice. Further,

---

3. Gallup, "What is the difference between a talent and a strength?" *Clifton-Strengths for Students.*

when we consider our strengths in tandem with a recognition of our *gifts,* those strengths can become even more powerful leadership tools. Strengths can be developed from any of the talents mentioned above, and they can also include things like being a great listener, learner, and critical thinker, among so many others. Importantly, we shouldn't feel discouraged that we lack certain strengths (even those we admire in others). No one does everything well.

UNIQUE GIFTEDNESS

You have been taught that you are a daughter of Heavenly Parents who love you, but it is hard to envision how heavenly beings can really know who you are amongst the billions of people currently living on this planet, right? You are told that you have unique talents, gifts, and strengths, but how is this possible?

Although I'm not an expert on the human body, I have done extensive reading on this individual uniqueness concept. It is compelling information that has convinced me of our distinctiveness. I'm going to get a little technical, but it is worth it.

The mystery is in what is called a synapse, which is a connection between two brain cells that enables neurons to communicate with one another.[4] Your behavior depends on these synapses that form interconnections among neurons in the brain. Synaptic connections start being formed forty-two days after you are conceived—when you are still in the womb.[5] In fact, you have about 100 billion when you are born. About sixty days before you are born, your neurons attempt to communicate and make connections with each other. Whenever a successful connection is made, a synapse is formed. And by the age of three each of your hundred billion neurons has formed 15,000 synaptic connections with other neurons (15,000 X 100 billion neurons). According to Gallup strengths experts, "Your pattern of threads, extensive, intricate, and unique, is woven."[6]

---

4.   Buckingham & Clifton, *Now, Discover Your Strengths.*
5.   Ibid.
6.   Ibid.

Because you cannot focus on all these connections, neglected ones start to break and you lose billions and billions of these synaptic connections. By the time you are sixteen, you have lost about half of this network, but that is okay because it needs to happen that way. After this you can still form some new connections if you need to learn how to cope with various circumstances, but for the most part your mental network is formed.

God has made it so that we have a lot more initial connections than we will ever need, and that many can be overwhelming. Hence, we must reduce the noise and focus on some more than others. Our genetic make-up and early childhood experiences work together to make some connections easier and stronger.[7] The ones we use more often become natural, while the billions of connections we ignore drop off our radar. This whole process helps us grow up and become adults. In fact, because of this process there is no way that any two people can ever be the same. With all these billions of neurons and synaptic connections being formed and withering away—influenced by our genetics and experiences—each of us emerges as a distinctly talented and gifted individual who reacts to the world in our own unique way.[8]

Our Heavenly Parents know each of you, and I believe they delight in your differences and how the combination of your spirit, body, background, challenges, and opportunities all come together into the grand creation of *you*. Sheri L. Dew wrote in her book, *Women and the Priesthood*, "Surely, then, our omniscient Father gave . . . His daughters the exact gifts, talents, privileges, responsibilities, opportunities, challenges, and divine errands we would need to help us stretch, struggle, serve, and eventually qualify for the gift of exaltation."[9] And, speaking specifically of the benefits of women together in the Relief Society, former First Counselor in the Young Women General Presidency Virginia H. Pearce has said, "Unity depends on our recognizing that each

---

7. Ibid.
8. Ibid.
9. Dew, *Women and the Priesthood*, 105.

of us has different talents and skills to contribute—different gifts—and that by uniting them, we can function as a whole."[10]

DISTRACTORS

Many things distract us from understanding, embracing, and utilizing our gifts, talents, and strengths. I will mention three here: misconceptions about humility, focusing on physical appearance, and restrictive social norms.

First, girls and women have been socialized into thinking they should be humble and not think about or talk about their talents. In fact, most of us are also socialized into thinking we are not good enough, so we don't even recognize our strengths. I have run workshops for women in many countries around the world, and no matter where I am, I observe the same reaction. I begin by asking women to reflect upon their talents and strengths and then discuss them with the person sitting next to them. This makes women very uncomfortable. They find it much easier to list and talk about their weaknesses versus their strengths. They feel like they are doing something wrong if they talk positively about themselves. Yet, when you know your distinctive gifts, talents, and strengths, you can contribute in better, more meaningful ways in this world. Humility just means being teachable. It does not mean that you should be small or insignificant. You can know your unique gifts and be teachable at the same time! In fact, some experts would say that being teachable—possessing *true* humility—means that we must acknowledge, accept, and apply the talents God has given us.[11]

Second, more and more young women believe that appearance is either a gift/talent or a curse/punishment. So many messages out there on social media, television, movies, and advertisements push you toward thinking this is the case. The pressure to obsess about how you look is strong, and negative body image is rampant because of this. As I will discuss in more detail later in the book, "We see

---

10. Dew and Pearce, *The Beginning of Better Days*, 12.
11. Smith, *Courage and Calling*, 39.

women, including ourselves, as bodies first and people second."[12] I don't believe that "looks" should be considered a gift, talent, curse, or punishment. This is hard to do, though, because we are socialized to look at girls' appearances even when they are babies. My two-year-old granddaughter is totally adorable, and it takes work for me not to focus on that! Time and energy wasted on worrying about our appearance leaves us with less time and energy to discover and develop our strengths.

Third, social norms often dictate many of our behaviors, and these can distract us from identifying and working on our talents. Many of these norms, found even in the Church, focus on gender—that boys and men should do certain things while girls and women should do others. Yet, some of your greatest natural talents could be in areas that are deemed masculine. For example, my daughter-in-law, Carlee, is absolutely amazing at building things. She finished their whole basement a few years ago with her toolbelt around her waist and my grandson following along. Sometimes girls and women don't even know what their talents are because social norms have limited their perceived options. In fact, some of the potential top-in-the-world pianists, soccer players, public speakers, scientists, innovators, and leaders never became the best because they didn't take lessons, join teams, take chances, enroll in courses, embrace opportunities, or let themselves dream.

STRATEGIES

You can use many approaches to discover your gifts, talents, and strengths, but I will share five specific strategies that I have used in coaching women. Doing the following will help you continue along your journey of preparing to lead:

1. **Create Lists:** In your journal (or the workbook that accompanies this book), create separate lists of your talents and

---

12. Kite & Kite, *More Than a Body: Your Body is an Instrument, Not an Ornament,* 6.

strengths that easily come to mind (review the definitions of talent and strength earlier in the chapter). Also, add a third list of the gifts you think you have been given that are connected to talents, strengths, confidence, and your overall journey of developing leadership.

2. **Expand Lists:** Add to these lists by asking yourself the following questions: What have others said I do well? What tasks or skills come easily to me (such as creating charts that motivate kids, convincing people to do things, repairing things around the house, teaching lessons)? What assignments do I look forward to digging into first thing in the morning? What activities make my heart leap?

3. **Ask Others:** Ask others who know you well (like parents, Young Women leaders, roommates, siblings, spouse) what they think are your top five strengths or talents. Then be careful not to respond with anything other than "thank you." Accept their feedback graciously! In addition, ask them what gifts they think you have been given that can put you in a position to become more influential. Record their responses in your journal.

4. **Expand Self-Understanding:** Complete self-evaluations and assessments that help you see your talents and strengths in different ways (Gallup *StrengthsFinder*, for example). Review any career or other types of assessments you did in middle school, high school, and college as you may see some patterns. Also, review past journals (if you have them) to see if there are clues there. Along the way, try new things so you can see if you have natural talents and interests in those areas.

5. **Seek for Spiritual Guidance:** Read, ponder, and pray about your patriarchal blessing. Record words, phrases, and thoughts about the talents and gifts discussed. If you haven't yet received your patriarchal blessing, take the necessary steps to do so. It can be a comfort and guide through so much of your life. Let God also tell you other talents that have not yet surfaced, so you can put yourself in situations that will help you learn, grow, and develop them. Be open to seeing and

learning about more of the gifts you have been given and how they relate to expanding your talents and strengths.

CONCLUSION

Church leaders have been vocal about the importance of using your gifts, talents, and strengths. For example, President Russell M. Nelson stated: "I urge you, with all the hope of my heart, to pray to understand *your spiritual gifts*—to cultivate, use, and expand them, even more than you ever have. You will change the world as you do so."[13] Likewise, President Henry B. Eyring of the First Presidency recently proclaimed, "You are daughters of a loving Heavenly Father, who sent you into the world with unique gifts that you promised to use to bless others."[14] Finally, Jean B. Bingham, the Relief Society General President, observed, "Women give of their talents and abilities in incredible and diverse ways. They make a huge difference in the lives of all those around them—in their families, their places of work, church, school, or wherever else they spend their time."[15] She also encouraged women to discover, develop, and use their gifts as well as to always remember "who gave them to us, and then use them for His purposes."[16]

Each of you has a part to play in His great plan, and you—with your unique brain, personality, and spirit—must be prepared to do your part. The Savior knows you, and He will help you. These are not ordinary times, and you are not ordinary women.[17] You are beloved daughters of Heavenly Parents, "with a divine nature and eternal destiny."[18] You are not alone. There are many around you who want you to be able to rise to His call, to use your gifts and strengths, and learn, lift, and lead.

---

13. Nelson, "Sisters' Participation in the Gathering of Israel," 69.
14. Eyring, "Sisters in Zion," 69.
15. Bingham, "Women of Covenant: The Importance of Seeking and Acting on Revelation," para. 12.
16. Ibid, para. 11.
17. Dalton, *No Ordinary Women*, 19.
18. "Young Women Theme," para. 1.

CHAPTER 7

Mindsets

"One of the greatest moments in anybody's developing experience is when [she] no longer tries to hide from [her]self but determines to get acquainted with [her]self as [s]he really is."

—NORMAN VINCENT PEALE[1]

A *mindset* is a set of attitudes someone possesses. It colors the way we look at the world. Mindsets are not just important in learning new skills and preparing to lead, but they can impact the way we think about nearly everything. As I work with girls and women on gaining confidence and finding and using their voices, I believe that understanding four specific mindsets is crucial. As we delve into the different ways of looking at life as viewed through a mindset lens, I hope you will see how much power there is in our mental attitudes.

First, psychologist Carol Dweck, author of *Mindset: The New Psychology of Success*,[2] focused her groundbreaking work on two specific mindsets: fixed and growth. Her work continues to impact educators, parents, and others. In fact, the growth mindset has influenced how I teach, train, develop, and educate people of all

---

1. Peale, "Believe in Yourself."
2. Dweck, *Mindset: The New Psychology of Success.*

ages. Overall, it is a difference between one's assumptions and beliefs around ability (fixed) versus effort (growth) or being (fixed) versus becoming (growth).

Second, two additional mindsets—the forgiveness and reflection mindsets—are also important to discuss when considering how you can prepare to influence. The poet Alexander Pope reportedly said, "To err is human; to forgive, divine." And author and psychotherapist Richard Carlson stated, "Reflection is one of the most underused yet powerful tools for success."[3] Your abilities and willingness to forgive and reflect are important competencies for becoming a leader in today's world.

FIXED MINDSET

The fixed mindset is not something you should aspire to possess. It is linked with a belief that individuals are either smart and talented, or they are not. It is "either/or" or "one or the other," marked by a belief that there is no way to change. When individuals believe that intelligence is carved in stone and can't be changed, they want to appear smart to others. This creates pressure to prove themselves over and over. They want success more than learning and growth. These individuals don't want to admit to or correct flaws or deficiencies. In fact, they stay clear of challenges because looking smart is more important than actually learning. If they fail, they don't want to try again because they believe failure is a sign of incompetence. People in the fixed mindset also tend to blame others a lot for their failures or, if they blame themselves, they go right to thoughts like "I am stupid" or "I suck." They also believe that *effort* is only for people who aren't "good enough."

So, when people are in the fixed mindset, they avoid challenges, give up easily, wonder why they should bother trying, believe talent is innate, assume that failure is proof that someone is not smart, and are threatened by others' success. People in this mindset often feel an entitlement that they deserve better (like better friends, a

---

3. Carlson, "Richard Carlson Quote."

better job, better parents, or a better apartment). This mindset limits achievement because everything is about the outcome or the result instead of the journey. So, if they fail, then the process or journey has been a waste. Those who lean more toward a fixed mindset look for friends and eventual spouses who make them feel superior, who worship them, make them feel perfect, and put them on a pedestal. Overall, a fixed-minded individual believes that the world needs to change around them instead of them changing, shifting, learning, and growing themselves. Overall, innate *ability* and a current state of *being* are what seem to be most important.

GROWTH MINDSET

On the other hand, as Professor Dweck[4] teaches, the growth mindset is based on the belief that intelligence can be learned and developed. It is an understanding that an individual's basic qualities can improve through *effort*, work, and support. Instead of focusing on their state of *being*, they are more interested in the process of *becoming*. Success is based on *effort* instead of fixed or natural *ability*. Basically, those who have stronger growth mindsets believe that they can develop their talents, capabilities, aptitudes, interests, and even temperaments. They embrace challenges, believe talent can be developed, view failure as a chance to grow, believe effort leads to success, are inspired by the success of others, and want to keep improving.

In fact, these individuals do not shy away from failure because they believe that it brings learning and they see the benefits of the journey. If they did have a painful experience with failure, it doesn't define them. Instead, it is a problem to be faced, resolved, and learned from. Because the journey is so important to them, they can love what they are doing even if they have difficulties. Growth-mindset individuals enjoy challenges and struggles, regardless of the outcome. They feel the desire to tackle problems, chart new courses, and work on important issues. Success comes when

---

4.   Dweck, *Mindset: The New Psychology of Success.*

they do their best, learn, change, grow, and improve.[5] Interestingly, setbacks can actually be motivating, educational, and sometimes even a wake-up call.

People in the growth mindset believe in change and love seeing others change, grow, and develop. These individuals think about what they can learn from experiences and how they can improve. Carol Dweck stated, "Effort is one of those things that gives meaning to life. Effort means you care about something, that something is important to you and you are willing to work for it."[6] For these individuals, their ideal friend or spouse would be someone who sees their faults, helps them work on them, challenges them to become better, and encourages them to learn new things. They surround themselves with others also trying to improve. Learning is the key focus of the growth mindset, as opposed to simply protecting fixed abilities.

Overall, studies have shown that people who lean toward a growth mindset are more likely to have "better self-esteem, confidence, relationships, self-efficacy, resilience, feelings of responsibility, and job performance; lower levels of stress, anxiety, insecurity, depression, and perfectionist tendencies; and higher levels of helpful vulnerability, life enjoyment, and drive for learning."[7] The growth mindset is obviously what we should strive for if we care about developing leadership traits and preparing for a future only God can see. However, depending on how each of us has been raised and our current environment, we may have developed fixed mindset patterns. According to Professor Dweck, "More and more research is suggesting that, far from being simply encoded in the genes, much of personality is a flexible and dynamic thing that changes over the lifespan and is shaped by experience."[8] So, the good news is that we can change and rewire ourselves toward a growth mindset.

---

5. Ibid.
6. Ibid.
7. Madsen, "Strengthen Your Growth Mindset: Using this Uncertain Time for Learning," para. 5.
8. Dweck, "Can Personality Be Changed? The Role of Beliefs in Personality and Change," 391–394.

FORGIVENESS MINDSET

In addition to understanding the difference between the fixed and growth mindsets, I want to focus on two more gospel principles that can also be seen as mindsets, or a set of attitudes we possess. First, our attitudes, tendencies, and habits toward becoming a generous and relentless forgiver can impact our leadership development journeys. Learning to better forgive ourselves and others is a powerful practice that can change lives, particularly our own. There are so many situations where we can offend and be offended. However, some of the most important work we can do in life is to heal relationships.

Did you know that more forgiving people tend to have better physical health, decreased blood pressure, fewer physician visits, lower stress, better healing from pain and illness, increased personal happiness, reduced anxiety and depression, and increased compassion?[9] Did you know that in workplaces there is a link between forgiveness and productivity, higher morale, increased satisfaction, and better working relationships?[10] Imagine how these findings can bring value into other settings as well, like school, church, home, and beyond.

Forgiving and then moving forward is the key. President M. Russell Ballard of the Quorum of the Twelve Apostles once stated: "Regardless of how hard you try, you can't change the past. What I want you to learn to do is look upstream. Watch for the things that are coming down the river of life that you can change and control."[11] And, Elder Jeffrey R. Holland, also of the Quorum of the Twelve Apostles, stated: "May I plead with us not to be hurt—and certainly not to feel envious—when good fortune comes to another person? We are not diminished when someone else is added upon. We are not in a race against each other to see who is the wealthiest or the most talented or the most beautiful or even the most blessed."[12]

---

9. Madsen, "Guest Op-ed: The Gift of Forgiveness."
10. Aquino, Grover, Goldman, and Folger, "When Push Doesn't Come to Shove: Interpersonal Forgiveness in Workplace Relationships."
11. Ballard, "Go for It!"
12. Holland, *To My Friends: Message of Counsel and Comfort*, 29.

As teen and young adult women, the world often feels upside down. However, I believe that if we all reach deep within ourselves and find ways to be more forgiving, we will be able to learn, grow, and contribute to God's work in more meaningful ways. Forgiveness is a mutually beneficial activity, and by practicing it we will find that lifting others lifts us.

REFLECTION MINDSET

Many years ago, leadership scholar Warren Bennis wrote something I've used in speeches for many years: "There are lessons in everything, and if you are fully deployed, you will learn most of them. Experiences aren't truly yours until you think about them, analyze them, examine them, question them, reflect on them, and finally understand them. The point . . . is to use your experiences rather than being used by them, to be the designer, not the design, so that experiences empower rather than imprison."[13]

Many people believe that experiences are what teach us important lessons. But it is not the experiences that truly teach us—it is the *reflection* on the experiences that teach us. Leadership development is all about learning, growth, and change, and it takes reflection to do that. Possessing a set of attitudes—a mindset—around embracing and respecting reflection has been strongly linked to leadership development.

In fact, I believe that you cannot truly develop as a leader unless you are open to ongoing, deep learning. You must let your experiences transform you. If you engage in this type of learning, which I believe comes from a growth mindset mentality, it can fundamentally change the way you see yourself, others, and the world around you. To do this, you must practice critical reflection, which means that you not only think about your experiences but that you also explore your underlying beliefs and assumptions and how they influence those experiences.[14]

---

13. Bennis, *On Becoming a Leader*, 92.
14. Madsen, "The Key to Leadership Development is Critical Reflection."

Frankly, this takes work. In fact, educator Robert Dilworth once stated: "It takes time and practice to unlock the ability to reflect. The art of critical reflection takes even longer, and some never get there. . . . When the reflection pushes to the deeper levels of self, it becomes possible to jettison dysfunctional assumptions and behaviors. Deep learning can then occur. It can become transformative learning."[15] If you can create deep reflection habits while you are young, you can harness learning from your experiences in better ways that will help you transform and become a stronger leader.

STRATEGIES

So, how can you strengthen your skills and aptitudes related to the growth, forgiveness, and reflection mindsets? I offer eight general strategies:

1. **Prioritize Hard Work:** Change your thinking patterns to link progress and success to effort, hard work, and "becoming," instead of existing ability, intellect, and "being." Hard work is at the core of accomplishments. Instead of thinking that either you are smart or you're not, recognize that intelligence can grow when exercised, just like a muscle.

2. **Be Brutally Honest with Yourself:** To make progress with improving who you are, you must embrace hard truths. You will need to explore what might trigger your fixed mindset (criticism, disagreements) and what brings out your growth mindset (learning environments, certain people). Practice being conscious when the triggers arise so you can focus on all three positive mindsets.

3. **Practice Learning from Mistakes:** Many people attempt to block out memories of their mistakes, but carefully observing yourself and others can teach you many lessons that can be applied in any setting and situation.

---

15. Dilworth, "Creating Opportunities for Reflection in Action Learning," para. 16.

As discussed in chapter 5, this includes learning to be okay with failure. Dealing with failure quickly—and then moving forward—can help you have more powerful growth experiences. Mistakes are our teachers.

4. **Seek Challenges:** Because of fear of failure, fixed mindset people shy away from challenges. If you have a growth mindset, challenges are viewed as developmental opportunities. Challenges can include being in situations where you may be offended or embarrassed, so cultivating the forgiveness and reflection mindsets can be helpful in ensuring you grow from these experiences.

5. **Develop a Habit of Being Positive and Optimistic:** People who are more optimistic tend to have more hope. Hope is a foundational element of a growth mindset because it focuses on possibility. Things that have shown to help increase optimism include reframing situations, making a list of blessings, becoming more grateful, and meditating and being more reflective.

6. **Embrace Change:** Change can be difficult for everyone, but shifting your mind to embrace changes in yourself, others, and circumstances can help you become more open to the many steps and phases in life that will prepare you to influence and impact. Remember that most growth is brought about by change.

7. **Forgive Freely:** To forgive freely you must understand more about forgiveness and why it matters. If you can analyze why you are feeling the way you do, then you can practice reframing through an empathic lens. Developing a forgiving heart can change your life. Forgiveness is letting go and frees us more than the person who has hurt us. Reflective journaling can help. Become a generous and relentless forgiver.

8. **Strengthen Reflection Skills:** Create a habit of thinking about each life experience and what you learned or can learn from it. Do this for positive as well as painful and challenging experiences. After having an experience, ask yourself

these three questions: What did I learn from this experience? How do I feel about it? If I had it to do all over again, what would I have said or done differently? Write your responses in a reflection journal or the workbook that accompanies this book. Discuss the learning experience with someone you trust.

Overall, shifting mindsets takes work and will surely take you out of your comfort zone. This sometimes means that you may become anxious and afraid. But consider this quote by President Thomas S. Monson: "My young brothers and sisters, don't take counsel of your fears. Don't say to yourselves, 'I'm not wise enough, or I can't apply myself sufficiently well to study this difficult subject or in this difficult field, so I shall choose the easier way.' I plead with you to tax your talent, and our Heavenly Father will make you equal to those decisions."[16] Working with your own mindsets will make a difference in your life.

CONCLUSION

Women with positive and powerful mindsets are needed. Elder Marvin J. Ashton, former member of the Quorum of the Twelve Apostles, made this powerful statement a few decades ago: "This is a day when serious minded, clear thinking women are needed to promote a climate of peace, harmony, and righteousness in community life. Let such women work together to create an atmosphere in which the problems of our society can be resolved by reason, respect, and concern for all people, and by esteem for that which has traditionally proved conducive to mankind's happiness and well-being. Let us remember that the woman whose life is well ordered may and should work for the benefit of both her community and her family."[17]

More recently, President Russell M. Nelson proclaimed: "Attacks against the Church, its doctrine, and our way of life are

---

16. Monson, "Life's Greatest Decisions," 4.
17. DeHoyos, *Stewardship—The Divine Order*, 105.

going to increase. Because of this, we need women who have a bed-rock understanding of the doctrine of Christ and who will use that understanding to teach and help raise a sin-resistant generation. We need women who can detect deception in all of its forms. We need women who know how to access the power that God makes available to covenant keepers and who express their beliefs with confidence and charity. We need women who have the courage and vision of our Mother Eve."[18]

Although each of us has our own journey in life, we all have God-given responsibilities to influence and impact in ways that these and other Church leaders have asserted. Christ has taught us that "faith without works is dead" (James 2: 26) and to "go, and do thou likewise" (Luke 10: 37). *Effort matters.* He also commands us to forgive those who have hurt or offended us: "Forgive us our debts, as we forgive our debtors" (Matthew 6:12). *Forgiveness matters.* And, throughout the scriptures our Savior and His disciples paused to ponder: "And again he stooped down, and wrote on the ground" (John 8:7) and "Mary kept all these things, and pondered them in her heart" (Luke 2:19). *Reflection matters.* Now is the time to start shifting our mindsets toward those that align with the attributes of our Savior. Grow, forgive, and reflect.

---

18. Nelson, "A Plea to My Sisters," 97.

CHAPTER 8

Education

"Prepare to do work of real worth for your fellowmen. . . . The critical difference between your just hoping for good things for mankind and your being able to do good things for mankind is education."

—PRESIDENT RUSSELL M. NELSON[1]

Earning college and university certificates and degrees is another step on your journey of preparing to lead. President Gordon B. Hinckley once stated: "Education is the key which will unlock the door of opportunity for you. . . . If you educate your mind and your hands, you will be able to make a great contribution to the society of which you are a part."[2] Similarly, he expressed, "The whole gamut of human endeavor is now open to women. There is not anything that you cannot do if you will set your mind to it. . . . You can include in the dream of the woman you would like to be a picture of one qualified to serve society and make a significant contribution to the world of which she will be a part."[3]

Learning and education have been central to the teachings of the Church since its restoration. In fact, President Brigham Young

---

1. Nelson, "Reflection and Resolution," para. 61.
2. Hinckley, "Inspirational Thoughts," para. 9
3. Hinckley, "How Can I Become the Woman of Whom I Dream?" 95.

was credited with making the following statements: "You educate a man; you educate a man. You educate a woman; you educate a generation." And, "If I had a choice of educating my daughters or my sons because of opportunity constraints, I would choose to educate my daughters." In more recent years, Elder Dieter F. Uchtdorf of the Quorum of the Twelve Apostles stated: "For members of the Church, education is not merely a good idea—it's a commandment."[4] And President Russell M. Nelson has declared: "Your mind is precious! It is sacred. Therefore, the education of one's mind is also sacred. Indeed, education is a religious responsibility."[5]

In your leadership preparation journey, pursuing and completing college certificates and degrees is foundational. This chapter first focuses on the research around the benefits you gain by attending and graduating from institutions of higher education. I then provide Church teachings on the topic, share some background about my own educational journey, and conclude with more of my favorite quotes.

BENEFITS OF HIGHER EDUCATION

The research is clear: getting a college education changes lives. However, young sisters in the Church still tell me that they have received mixed messages about the role that college should play for them personally. For example, young women have told me that they have been advised by their parents, friends, or Church leaders that to be a "good Latter-day Saint mother" they don't need to go to college. This is simply not true. Hundreds of studies have found that a college/university education (particularly at the bachelor's degree attainment level or higher) helps women in all areas of their lives. In fact, when women earn college degrees, they are better able to realize their own potential for positive influence and contributions to home, society, workplace, and beyond.

In reviewing hundreds of studies about the value of higher education for women and men, I have identified key benefits in

---

4. "Education is a Commandment," para. 2.
5. Ibid., para. 15.

six areas: parenting, civic and community engagement, health and well-being, self-development, intellectual development, and societal and economic outcomes. Of course, it is important to note that people do many of these things without degrees, but the research is clear that, generally speaking, this is the case. And higher education strengthens knowledge and skills so that people become even more effective and receive even more benefits.

Parenting

There are many reasons a college education can contribute to better parenting. Educated mothers are more likely to give birth to healthier babies since they are less likely to consume alcohol or smoke.[6] By elementary school, children of educated mothers and fathers are more prepared academically. College degree earners tend to spend more time reading to their children, which is linked to academic success.[7] In addition, children whose parents are college educated seek for higher degrees, have less self-doubt, understand more about how to navigate the college process, and are less than half as likely to drop out before their second year.[8] Preparing your children for a successful life is a critical piece of parenting.

Civic and Community Engagement

Adults who have gone to college are more likely to engage in their community and be more civically active. For example, significantly more people with at least some college education vote compared to those with only a high school diploma.[9] And women who have more education are more likely to volunteer in school as well

6. Boardman, Powers, Padilla, and Hummer, "Low Birth Weight, Social Factors, and Developmental Outcomes among Children in the United States."
7. Ma, Pender, and Welch, "Education Pays 2019: The Benefits of Higher Education for Individuals and Society."
8. Pascarella, and Terenzini, "How College Affects Students: A Third Decade of Research."
9. Gramlich, "What the 2020 Electorate Looks Like by Party, Race and Ethnicity, Age, Education, and Religion."

as many other settings.[10] One of the reasons is that college students tend to have greater opportunities to learn more about and spend time working with non-profit organizations and other community-based settings through internships and course-related service learning. Also, more educated people are also more likely to donate blood, give to charities, and invest in community-building in a variety of ways. Overall, higher education clearly translates to a more prepared and conscientious civic participant and community volunteer.[11]

Health and Well-Being

Having a college degree is associated with a healthier lifestyle, which impacts the health and well-being of families as well. Educated people tend to exercise more consistently and vigorously,[12] have lower rates of smoking,[13] are less often overweight or obese (which has been linked to less disease and health risks), and have lower rates of alcohol abuse-dependency, lower cholesterol levels, and higher dietary fiber intake.[14] Other researchers have reported that college-educated individuals have increased levels of life satisfaction, overall happiness,[15] increased resilience, and experience less depression and suicide.[16] They also tend to have more resources like employer-provided health insurance, access to health care, retirement plans, discretionary savings, and more extensive social-support networks.

---

10. "Volunteering in the United States, 2015," US Bureau of Statistics.
11. Madsen, Hanewicz, Thackeray, and King, "A Glimpse at Women and Higher Education in Utah."
12. Ma, Pender, and Welch, "Education Pays 2019: The Benefits of Higher Education for Individuals and Society."
13. Ibid.
14. "Goals for the Common Good: Exploring the Impact of Education," Measure of America and United Way.
15. Pew Research Center, "How Americans View Their Jobs."
16. Phillips and Hempstead, "Differences in U.S. Suicide Rates by Educational Attainment, 2000–2014."

Intellectual and Cognitive Development

As you can probably guess, you get smarter when you attend college and obtain degrees. Your knowledge grows and your brain develops. In addition to the knowledge you get from the field you major in (like business, behavioral science, science, information technology, or secondary education), you also gain understanding and competencies in things like communication, creative and critical thinking abilities, lifelong learning capabilities, verbal and writing skills, interpersonal and teamwork abilities, quantitative and analysis skills, reflective judgment, principled moral reasoning, the ability to integrate ideas and concepts, content knowledge in various fields, factual knowledge, reading comprehension, skills in comparing and analyzing information, and the capacity to learn effectively on your own. All of these are important for meaningful contributions and leadership in any setting, including in the home, workplace, politics, church, and community.

Self-Development

Higher education also helps women develop themselves in a variety of ways. Many courses influence and promote a student's self-understanding through teaching elements related to independence, interpersonal relationships, leadership development, problem solving, decision making, confronting prejudice, and developing moral and ethical standards. Research shows that college students experience positive changes in thinking, social skills, attitude and value refinement, self-concept and self-esteem, diversity and inclusion understanding, and an increased interest in culture, the arts, social issues, and world affairs. These changes have been shown to be sustainable well into the adult years and typically continue into old age.

Societal and Economic Outcomes

Communities and societies that have higher levels of education are safer. For example, for every year of increase in the average schooling level within a community, there is a 30 percent decrease in murder.[17] Education also provides the avenue out of poverty and encourages people to invest in their communities. In fact, education is the single most important factor in whether or not a person will live in poverty. People who have more education earn more money. This has been shown in studies throughout the decades and still applies today. Education also has an impact on job opportunities, employment and occupational status, and high-quality health insurance and other benefits.[18] Overall, adults with bachelor's degrees can expect to make more than a million dollars more in their lifetime career than adults with high school diplomas.[19]

Overall, there are so many reasons for young women to go to college, and I encourage them to jump in immediately after high school. If you do take a break, return to college as soon as possible. Don't put college on the back burner. Life always "happens," and if you don't take the opportunities to continue your education now, you may not be prepared for that future only God can see for you. Education will benefit you in all areas of your life as you get older, and it is an important foundation for positively influencing others throughout your life.

CHURCH TEACHINGS

Why is education so important in The Church of Jesus Christ of Latter-day Saints? I have studied this question for years, and this is what I have discovered. Since "the glory of God is intelligence" (D&C 93:36), then gaining intelligence is central to our existence.[20] Because "the objective of all people is to continuously strive to become like Him" and "learning is essential for salvation," "God has made education a divine commandment." As "education is one of life's preeminent purposes and has enduring eternal value that

---

17. "Goals for the Common Good: Exploring the Impact of Education," Measure of America and United Way.
18. Ma, Pender, and Welch, "Education Pays 2019: The Benefits of Higher Education for Individuals and Society."
19. Pak & Kroes, "Lifetime Value of a College Degree."
20. "Education," in *Gospel Topics*.

transcends death," life is a "school to develop understanding through both study and experience."[21] Further, the Lord has instructed us to "seek learning, even by study and also by faith" (D&C 88:118).

The Church of Jesus Christ of Latter-day Saints offers several unique educational opportunities in both religious and secular education. Many high-school aged students attend seminary, while those ages eighteen to thirty can attend Institute of Religion classes. The Church Educational System promotes higher education through different church-sponsored colleges and universities such as Brigham Young University, BYU—Hawaii, BYU—Idaho, Ensign College, BYU—Pathway Worldwide, vocational training opportunities through Deseret Industries, and other programs. Wards and stakes can also offer self-reliance groups—which combine "practical courses" with "spiritual benefits"—in topics such as Emotional Resilience, Personal Finances, Starting and Growing My Business, Find a Better Job, and Education for Better Work. I'd be surprised if the Church's educational offerings didn't continue to grow and develop in the coming years.

Latter-day Church leaders have also provided their encouragement for women to seek education. In fact, Elder Dallin H. Oaks of the Quorum of the Twelve Apostles said, "We make no distinction between young men and young women in our conviction about the importance of an education and in our commitment to providing that education."[22] President Gordon B. Hinckley once stated, "The pattern of study you establish during your formal schooling will in large measure affect your lifelong thirst for knowledge." He counseled us to get all the education that we possibly can and to sacrifice anything that is needed to make this happen. In speaking specifically to women, President Thomas S. Monson taught that "a mother's education level has a profound influence on the educational choices of her [children]" and that a mother's education can hold the "key to halt [the] poverty cycle." Likewise, Mary N. Cook,

---

21. "Latter-day Saints and Education: An Overview," *Newsroom*, para. 2.
22. Oaks, "Women and Education," para. 7.

former First Counselor in the Young Women General Presidency, stated: "Bless your children and your future home by learning as much as you can now."[23]

According to President Henry B. Eyring of the First Presidency, "The Lord and His Church have always encouraged education to increase our ability to serve Him and our Heavenly Father's children. For each of us, whatever our talents, He has service for us to give. And to do it well always involves learning, not once or for a limited time, but continually. . . . It is clear that putting spiritual learning first does not relieve us from learning secular things. On the contrary, it gives our secular learning purpose and motivates us to work harder at it. . . . Remember, you are interested in education, not just for mortal life but for eternal life."[24]

Two specific quotes always bring a smile to my face. First, in 1992, Church author and member of the General Young Women Board Marie Hafen stated: "Anyone who uses Church teachings as an excuse for thinking women should not wholeheartedly seek an education does not understand what the Church teaches."[25] This is so true! And second, many years ago Elder Richard G. Scott of the Quorum of the Twelve Apostles answered a question from someone at one of the Church universities on how to advise women who believe they cannot justify the cost of completing their education when they plan to stay home with their children. It was recorded that "Elder Scott seemed a little surprised by the question but responded instantly: 'Please, open their eyes. . . . A mother has got to be brilliantly educated in today's world. One of the greatest gifts that can be given to today's children is a mother in the home who is well-educated.'"[26]

Finally, when serving in the Quorum of the Twelve Apostles, President Russell M. Nelson stated: "Our Creator expects His children

---

23. Cook, "Seek Learning: You Have a Work to Do," 120.
24. Eyring, "Education for Real Life," 18.
25. Hafen, "Celebrating Womanhood," para. 35.
26. Hurley, "What if 'Plan A' Doesn't Work? Helping Female Students Navigate an Uncertain Life Course," 78.

everywhere to gain an education as a personal endeavor. . . . When you leave this frail existence, your material possessions will remain here, but the Lord has declared that the knowledge you acquire here will rise with you in the resurrection. . . . In light of this celestial perspective, if you impulsively drop out or otherwise cut short your education, you would not only disregard a divine decree but also abbreviate your own eternal potential." He continued, "So my counsel then—and now—is to continue your education, wherever you are, whatever your interest and opportunity may be. Determine how you can best serve your family and society and prepare well."[27]

MY EXPERIENCE

While I was growing up, I watched my father go back to college for his master's degree when I was seven or eight years old. He made it a priority even though he had young children at home. He knew it was important for him, the family, and the Lord. When I was about sixteen years old my father finished a doctoral degree in educational psychology from BYU. In both cases, we moved to Provo during the summers so he could attend face-to-face classes. I still remember wandering around campus, swimming in the large indoor pool, and attending some summer programs. Through these experiences, I knew education was important. Even though my mother did not finish college—she married one semester before she finished her RN—she worked hard to support him. My father was a seminary and institute teacher, and my mother always took institute classes and studied and learned constantly.

In addition, my patriarchal blessing made it clear to me that formal education was to be part of my preparation in life. I know that it is not necessarily mentioned in everyone's blessing, but I'm grateful it was in mine, as I was able to make it a priority early on. I always knew this would mean doing the "and" and not the "either/or," as I discussed earlier. I gave birth to my first child (Michael) after I finished my bachelor's degree at BYU, but my heart yearned

---

27. Nelson, "Education: A Righteous Responsibility," para. 12.

to return sooner than later. After a few years and the birth of my second son (Brian), my husband graduated with his MBA and we moved to Portland, Oregon. I was immediately able to attend Portland State University part-time and complete my master's degree in two years. I was blessed to be able to teach piano lessons for extra money and traded lessons for daycare with friends in my ward a few afternoons each week so I could attend classes. In addition, my mother and mother-in-law came out to help watch the boys for a few weeks for two summers so I could attend full-time during a high-intensive one-month special summer session.

After I completed my master's degree, my husband's employment took us to Southern California, where we lived for five years. During these years I gave birth to two more children (Staci and Scott), and then we moved to White Bear Lake, Minnesota. During these Minnesota years I was able to start and finish a doctoral program in human resource development from the University of Minnesota. When I began my coursework, I had four children who ranged from ages three to eleven. I was prompted to enroll in a program that was flexible and would work with parenting responsibilities, as I wanted to continue to be the primary caregiver. It got tricky at times, but I knew it was right.

Sadly, on occasion, a few people in my ward were judgmental about my choices to continue my education. They had no clue what the Lord wanted me to do. They had no idea what future God was preparing for me. It was between me and the Lord, and my husband also had confirmations from the Lord that this was right. I remember one day a sister from my ward asked me why I was "leaving my children" to get my advanced degree. She felt that I was disadvantaging my children by "leaving them" a few evenings a week and that I was most likely "ignoring" them during the day when I was studying. The second time she said these things to me, I paused for a moment and then looked directly in her eyes and said, "I'm working on my PhD because God told me to!" That ended the conversation, and I've used that phrase ever since.

Each of you has your own unique journey that you will need to navigate. You must receive your own personal revelation to guide your decisions. However, I truly believe that any journey that includes attending and completing formal college—certificates and degrees—will become a critical life step toward preparing to lead. Going to college earlier rather than later in life will help arm you with more knowledge, tools, and strategies to serve the Lord in impactful ways. Yet, for women who were not able to attend or finish postsecondary education in young adulthood, don't dismay. I encourage you to return. Furthering your college education at any time during your life's journey will help improve what you can do and how you can serve.

CONCLUSION

As I do the work I do, Doctrine and Covenants 130:18–21 often comes to mind: "Whatever principle of intelligence we attain unto in this life, it will rise with us in the resurrection. And if a person gains more knowledge and intelligence in this life through his diligence and obedience than another, he will have so much the advantage in the world to come."

In her popular 2017 BYU devotional speech, Dr. Eva Witesman said: "Sisters, never question the value of your education or wonder whether you will have an opportunity to learn and use the knowledge you have gained. God knows you, and even though you may not yet know His plans, He knows the end from the beginning. He is preparing and qualifying you for the work He wants you to do. He will continually guide you to ways in which your knowledge and skills can be of benefit to yourself, your family, your community, and His kingdom."[28]

I wholeheartedly agree with Dr. Witesman and all the Church leaders I have cited in this chapter. As sisters in The Church of Jesus Christ of Latter-day Saints, you are commanded to get all the education you can so that you can prepare for that future only God can see for you. I didn't know why I felt prompted to continue my

---

28. Witesman, "Women and Education: 'A Future Only God Could See for You,'" 6.

education through the years, but I felt the promptings and I acted. It took confidence, perseverance, and faith. And now, I can look back on my life thus far and see how the puzzle pieces have all fit together. I am deeply humbled by the way my Heavenly Parents have been able to use me to further their work. Some may continue to judge me and my choices, but the only judge that matters is my Savior. He is my light. He is the center of my life, and what *He* thinks is what matters most. Prayerfully seek your own inspiration and use your mind, choices, voice, and energy to make a difference in this world.

CHAPTER 9

Purpose and Callings

"For each individual there is a specific call—a defining purpose or mission, a reason for being. Every individual is called of God to respond uniquely through service in the world. . . . He calls us all to follow him, and once we accept that call, each of us is honored with a unique call that is an integral part of what it means to follow him."[1]

—GORDON T. SMITH

I have found that nearly all Latter-day Saint women strongly believe that mothering—defined most often as raising and nurturing children—is the greatest and most important calling they can have in life. I wholeheartedly agree. Yet even though the quote I used to begin this chapter talks about "a specific call," I believe that God has many life callings for each one of us. I do not believe that mothering is your *only* calling or purpose in life. We can all have multiple purposes; embracing one does not necessarily mean excluding another. Because mothering has most likely been discussed at length throughout your life thus far, I will not focus on it in this chapter. However, I do want to be clear that I personally believe that mothering is my greatest calling.

---

1. Smith, *Courage and Calling*, 9.

People are drawn to finding meaning in their lives. In fact, well over a decade ago, a *USA Today* poll found that if people could ask God just one question, most would want to know, "What's my purpose in life?"[2] Researchers[3] have found that people yearn to do work—paid or unpaid in any setting, including the home—that is needed, meaningful, makes a difference, and helps them experience a sense of purpose and calling in their lives. People want to believe there is something special within them and that they have some type of life mission to discover and fulfill. I would guess that this is true for anyone reading this book as well. You are most likely unsure at this point about what your purpose or callings might look like, but I expect, however, you still feel driven to prepare for that "future greater than anything you can imagine."[4] This chapter will lay the foundation for discovering your purpose and callings.

SETTING THE STAGE

Purpose and calling can be incredibly powerful, particularly for women. I know that I feel called to do work as a daughter, mother, spouse, Church member, professor, writer, community and social justice advocate, and women's leadership scholar. This sense of calling gets me up each morning with energy, drives my daily decisions, and brings me peace when I face challenges. Because I firmly believe I am doing God's will in my home, workplace, and community, I feel hope. Although I am far from perfect and have endured painful struggles throughout my life, this meaning, purpose, and call propels me forward. I truly believe that I am called by God to do the work I do, and that includes a call to write this book.

I tell you this so you will understand how deeply and personally I feel about girls and women finding the various "callings" they have in life to serve, influence, and impact others in distinctive, beautiful,

---

2. Brennfleck and Brennfleck, *Live Your Calling*, 3.
3. Smith, *Courage and Calling*, 31; Steger, Pickering, Shin, and Dik, "Calling in Work: Secular or Sacred?"
4. Uchtdorf, "Living the Gospel Joyful," 121.

and bold ways. I truly believe that when sisters seek and discover their callings, they will find opportunities to serve our Heavenly Father that they may not have considered before.

Identifying, clarifying, and applying your calling is not a one-time event but a journey that will continue throughout your life. It is an ongoing process of thinking about your purpose, the meaning of what you are doing, and the changes you need to make depending on the circumstances that arise in your life. Calls may shift based on whether you are prepared with the needed confidence, education, mindsets, identity, and recognition of your gifts, talents, and strengths. They may also be based on what experiences you have had, what opportunities you have embraced, and your aspirations and ambitions. As well-known American poet Oliver Wendell Holmes once wrote, "Every calling is great when greatly pursued."[5]

DESCRIPTIONS

What does *calling* mean? You have probably already discovered that I'm not talking about a formal calling that you may receive from a Church leader. The term "calling" was created in 1522 by the German theologian Martin Luther. His view, which was different from that of the Catholic Church at the time, was that everyone—not just religious leaders—had a call or callings from God. He believed that both religious and occupational work (paid jobs) were important to God.[6] Martin Luther thought that this sense of being called could help motivate people to serve their neighbors and communities more effectively. Calling has often been used interchangeably with the concept of "vocation," which involves living a life of meaning and purpose.[7]

---

5. Holmes, "Quotable Quotes," para. 1.
6. Oates, Hall, Anderson, and Willingham, "Pursuing Multiple Callings: The Implications of Balancing Career and Motherhood for Women and the Church."
7. Madsen, "Leadership Responsibility and Calling: The Role of Calling in a Woman's Choice to Lead," in *Responsible Leadership: Realism and Romanticism*.

You may have already noticed that I'm also using the word *purpose* in this chapter. Is there a difference between calling and purpose? The dictionary defines purpose as "something set up as an object or end to be attained; a subject under discussion or an action in course of execution; by intent."[8] So purpose could be viewed as an intentional act toward a common end. And calling, according to the description above, could be viewed as our own unique contributions toward that purpose or goal. I think calling and purpose together can be powerful.

WHAT MATTERS

As a woman, I admit that many influences inhibit girls' and women's growth toward preparing for and developing leadership abilities. Some examples include the way we are socialized toward following instead of leading, the cultural norms around us that say leaders should act and behave in masculine ways, the limited expectations others may have for us in terms of education or career, and the fear of judgment from others around what young women and sisters in the Church are "supposed" to do. These all dictate how we prepare and contribute our efforts, both in The Church of Jesus Christ of Latter-day Saints and in the world. Yet, I believe—after decades of feeling restless, unsettled, and even "lost" in some ways myself—that our feelings and reactions could be a sign that God needs us to show up in new and more authentic ways. However, it will take work to figure out how.

Listening to the Lord is the only way we can uncover that future only God can see for us. I love Mother Teresa's famous statement: "Very often I feel like a little pencil in God's Hands. He does the writing, He does the thinking, He does the movement, I have only to be the pencil."[9] We need to let Him write, think, and move us, but sometimes it is harder than it sounds. So, what should we consider as we think about our callings?

---

8. Merriam-Webster OnLine, s.v. "Purpose."
9. Teresa and Kolodiejchuk, *Mother Teresa: Come Be My Light: The Private Writings of the Saint of Calcutta*, 363.

First, the way we look at what we choose to do in life is so important. Author and speaker Joan Borysenko shared the following story: "A man saw three fellows laying bricks at a new building: He approached the first and asked, 'What are you doing?' Clearly irritated, the first man responded, 'What the heck do you think I'm doing? I'm laying these darn bricks!' He then walked over to the second bricklayer and asked the same question. The second responded, 'Oh, I'm making a living.' He approached the third bricklayer with the same question, 'What are you doing?' The third looked up, smiled and said, 'I'm building a cathedral.'"[10] Our attitudes and perspectives matter.

Second, the spiritual component of discovering calling is crucial. Church doctrine clearly outlines that even before we were born, we made promises to the Lord about some of the work we would do on this earth. Elaine S. Dalton, former Young Women General President, believes that "As we increase in our discipleship, we will become a greater force for good in the world. Never before has there been a time of such limitless opportunity to connect with others in the world—to serve, to testify, and to make a difference. Having faith in the Savior and purifying our lives enables us to have the constant companionship of the Holy Ghost, and through that power we may accomplish the great things we have been prepared and positioned on this earth to do."[11] Our spirituality matters.

Third, understanding more about who we are helps. Sheri L. Dew, former counselor in the Relief Society General Presidency, stated, "Perhaps nothing affects our ability to become who we're capable of becoming more than does knowing who we are, who we have always been, how real our divine potential is, and that we each have a divine errand—meaning that we have come to this earth with a mission to perform. Our errands are all different. Your life's mission is not mine, and mine is not yours. You are accountable for those things which long ago were expected of you

---

10. Borysenko, "Proverbial Wisdom."
11. Dalton, *No Ordinary Women*, 64.

just as are those we sustain as prophets and apostles!"[12] So, what do you long for? What are the desires of your heart? The desires of our heart matter to the Lord. One author stated, "When we are right with God and genuinely long to respond fully to him in a way that is consistent with his call in our lives, then we must acknowledge the desires that he has placed in our hearts."[13] Understanding who we are matters.

Finally, whatever we feel our call is, we need to remember this: "Our longing for meaningful work . . . must be framed in the context of that which is good, noble and excellent, that which enables us to bring pleasure to our Maker, that which we can say with genuine passion that we do 'as to the Lord.'"[14] Because we have the power to change the world. Our attitudes and perspectives matter, our spirituality matters, and understanding who we are matters.

POSITIONS AND PLACES

One Christian author discussed three levels of calls that he experienced: a general call to follow Christ; a specific call or mission unique to each person; and immediate calls that may come in moments, days, weeks, and even months.[15] These different calls could show up in a variety of positions and places.

Home and Family

We can identify various callings in our own homes that may emerge in many ways. For example, during your teen years you may feel called to be a peacemaker in your home or to be a steady influence for good among your siblings. In fact, I have witnessed young women who have done the work of saving souls in their own homes. You can feel called to be a spouse and mother and/or you could feel

---

12. Dew, *Women and the Priesthood*, 32.
13. Smith, *Courage and Calling*, 40.
14. Ibid., 22.
15. Ibid., 10.

called to take on caregiving and other support roles for your parents or other extended family members. These are just a few of many ways you could be called in your home and family.

Church

We also have formal and informal callings in the Church. Being someone who can be a tender mercy to others—a gift of the Spirit—can be a calling. President Henry B. Eyring of the First Presidency stated: "The Spirit can then guide what you think, what you say, and what you do to nurture people so the Lord may pour knowledge, truth, and courage upon them."[16] Formal callings in the Church can also be part of our larger life call as well. For example, serving in a Young Women, Primary, or Relief Society presidency could be something the Lord planned for you to do to contribute and serve, but also to learn leadership. All of us are asked to minister, and while this may seem like a "small" calling, according to Alma 37:6 "by small and simple things are great things brought to pass."

Community

You may feel called to do community work or to advocate for people with fewer advantages. You may feel promptings to use your voice to change things in your area or to lead volunteer efforts. Earlier chapters provide many ideas of ways you can prepare to lead—all of which could be part of your purpose and calling. In a 2020 presentation, Sharon Eubank, a member of the Relief Society General Presidency and the director of Latter-day Saint Charities, encouraged individuals, "Don't wait to be the change that you seek. . . . I don't ever want to wait for somebody else to organize something or plan something. I'll be the one."[17] We can do so much good in our own communities and inspire others to join in.

---

16. Eyring, "Women and Gospel Learning in the Home," 59.
17. Eubank, "The Status of Women Worldwide" (Speech, Utah Women's Leadership Speaker and Dialogue Series, Utah Valley University, Orem, February 19, 2020).

Workplace

Paid work can also be related to God's calling for us. As I mentioned, I feel called by God to do the work I do. I do get paid for some of it, but I volunteer a great deal of my time. When I speak and teach, I know at least some people are changed for the better. Even research confirms workplaces benefit when their leaders and employees feel called to be there.[18] As you have various paid jobs throughout your life, pay attention to which aspects of each job speak to you. This will help you refine your calling and be prepared for God's guidance.

Whatever we do to pursue our calls, let's remember these two things: First, let's not judge the decisions of other sisters. We don't know what God's call is for the sister who lives next door or a sister who lives in another state or country. A woman's call from God is her own. And second, pursuing a call may put you out of your comfort zone. However, Audre Lord stated, "You have a choice. You can throw in the towel or you can use it to wipe the sweat off your face. When I dare to be powerful, to use my strength in the service of my vision, then it becomes less important whether I am afraid."

STRATEGIES

Although there are many ways to unearth your purpose and callings, I will share a few ideas. Some of the strategies I've shared in previous chapters will also help you (such as strengthening your confidence, enhancing your growth mindset, and discovering your gifts, talents, and strengths).

1. **Seek Personal Revelation:** Reading, pondering, and praying about your patriarchal blessing will help. If you haven't received one yet, I encourage you to start your

---

18. Madsen, "Leadership Responsibility and Calling: The Role of Calling in a Woman's Choice to Lead," in *Responsible Leadership: Realism and Romanticism.*

preparations and get it scheduled. It can be a powerful guide in your life. Studying your blessing while thinking about your potential purpose and callings can help. Your blessing will either directly mention or provide hints toward your calls. Remember to think about this in terms of what you've already discovered about your distinctive gifts, talents, and strengths.

2. **Continue to Journal:** If you are following my suggestions and strategies from past chapters, you will have been journaling, and I recommend that you continue. Writing helps you think better, clarify more effectively, and remember the inspiration you receive along the way. Insights will come if you let yourself embrace the journey. Whether in a lovely bound book, in the notes on your phone, or the workbook that accompanies this book, recording your thoughts and ideas will bring clarity.

3. **Explore Potential Efforts, Initiatives, and Causes:** Look around for issues and projects that seem interesting, exciting, and intriguing to you. Reading your old diaries or journals can also help you remember what issues or topics seem to connect with your head, heart, and hands, along with your talents and strengths. Whatever the initiative or cause, it should allow you to use your voice, competencies, ambitions, and skills in various ways.

4. **Identify and Interpret the Call:** You should be ready now to identify and interpret at least one immediate call. As part of this process, you can obtain more information, continue to consider your gifts, seek out guidance from others, attend workshops or events that could provide clarity, and continue pondering and praying.[19]

5. **Pursue Your Call:** Open yourself to opportunities and seek out ways to get involved in areas that are aligned with a call

---

19. Tunheim and Goldschmidt, "Exploring the Role of Calling in the Professional Journeys of College Presidents."

or callings that you feel drawn to or guided toward. Initial engagement will allow you to identify and interpret your call, but it can also help you develop leadership through becoming involved with important initiatives. This is *action*. Step forward to engage!

CONCLUSION

Educator and author Parker Palmer wrote, "Our deepest calling is to grow into our own authentic self-hood, whether or not it conforms to some image of who we ought to be. As we do so, we will not only find the joy that every human being seeks—we will also find our path of authentic service in the world."[20] And as American writer and theologian Frederick Buechner stated, true vocation joins self and service in "the place where your deep gladness meets the world's deep need."[21] Finally, writer Gordon T. Smith shared this: "It takes courage to pursue our vocation, the courage to be—the courage to be true to who we are, even if it means living on the edge, living with risk, living with less security and less influence and less power—because to pursue our vocation means that we have chosen the way that is true to who we are, true to ourselves, true to our call."[22]

We were born at this very time for a specific reason. Uncovering our callings is part of our journey. As we feel called, we are more likely to step forward to influence and lead in powerful ways. With purpose and calling in hand, I believe you can be unstoppable in doing God's work.

---

20. Palmer, *Let Your Life Speak*, 16.
21. Buechner, *Wishful Thinking: A Seeker's ABC*, 119.
22. Smith, *Courage and Calling*, 123.

CHAPTER 10

Identity

"Latter-day Saint women draw strength and inspiration from their identity: they understand themselves to be daughters of God with a purpose in life, and they strive to cultivate the attributes of divinity—such as holiness, wisdom and charity—within themselves. . . . Through collaborative and unique efforts, they. . . . provide indispensable contributions at home, at church and in the community."[1]

—NEWSROOM, THE CHURCH OF JESUS CHRIST OF LATTER-DAY SAINTS

When you read the Young Women theme, you'll notice that much of it focuses on what you should *do,* while only the first sentence highlights who you *are*—your innate identity: "I am a beloved daughter of heavenly parents, with a divine nature and eternal destiny."[2] This is important, as knowing who you are—and believing it—can change everything for you. As I said in the introduction

---

1. "Women in the Church," in *Newsroom,* para. 1.
2. "Young Women Theme," para. 1.

of this book, I have been concerned for years about a gap in the Church between *hearing* and *reciting* doctrinal truths versus actually *believing* and *knowing* them.

According to various dictionaries, identity is 1) "the distinguishing character or personality of an individual,"[3] 2) "who a person is, or the qualities of a person or group that make them different from others,"[4] and 3) "the condition of being oneself or itself, and not another."[5] It is the essence of who we perceive ourselves to be. Knowing who we are is at the core of believing we have worth, understanding that we have a purpose and calling, and embracing our unique gifts, talents, and strengths.

As sisters in the Church, deep identity work needs to be connected to our relationship with God and how we believe He sees us. According to well-known Church leader and author Sheri L. Dew, the first step in "understanding how God sees His daughters—and the first step in coming to understand the privileges women have in God's kingdom—is understanding who we are, who we have always been, and who we may ultimately become."[6] This chapter explores identity more generally and then will focus specifically on leadership identity. If we know who we are and are aware of our purpose and callings, our leadership identity can better emerge in ways that will help us serve the Lord.

AN ESSENTIAL CHARACTERISTIC

"The Family: A Proclamation to the World" states the following: "All human beings—male and female—are created in the image of God. Each is a beloved spirit son or daughter of heavenly parents, and, as such, each has a divine nature and destiny. Gender is an essential characteristic of individual premortal, mortal, and eternal identity and purpose."[7] Let's read that last line once again: "Gender

---

3.   Merriam-Webster OnLine, s.v. "identity."
4.   Cambridge Dictionary OnLine, s.v., "identity."
5.   Dictionary.com OnLine, s.v., "identity."
6.   Dew, *Women and the Priesthood*, 47.
7.   "The Family: A Proclamation to the World," para. 2.

is an essential characteristic of individual premortal, mortal, and eternal identity and purpose."[8]

For decades I have studied gender research exploring the differences between men and women in terms of genetics, socialization, and choices. Gender influences nearly everything. And honestly, sometimes I think it would be easier to be a man—the world is not always kind to women! But when I truly ponder the role of women in these latter days, I feel honored to be trusted by the Lord to be one. Elder David A. Bednar of the Quorum of the Twelve Apostles said: "[Gender] in large measure defines who we are, why we are here upon the earth, and what we are to do and become. For divine purposes, male and female spirits are different, distinctive, and complementary. . . . The unique combination of spiritual, physical, mental, and emotional capacities of both males and females were needed to implement the plan of happiness"[9] Yes, men and women are different, but it is also true that no two women are the same either, and we each have our own unique purpose and callings.

WOMEN NEED WOMEN

As we already discussed, our identity is deeply connected to our gender. In fact, what we see women doing around us strongly impacts what we see ourselves doing in the future. We form our aspirations, ambitions, and goals most often by watching our mothers, sisters in our wards and stakes, our female teachers, and women we see in the community, on television, in the movies, and communicating on social media. In fact, we imagine our future possibilities by watching those of our own gender because, again, gender is vital to who we are.

Girls and women need to see faithful, strong, and competent women around them to envision what they can become in the future themselves. Author Wendy Ulrich wrote: "We do need women of power as a Church and I need to see powerful women to become one

---

8. Ibid.
9. Bednar, "Marriage Is Essential to His Eternal Plan," 83.

myself. We all, male and female need mentoring, experience, and the opportunity to learn from both failure and success as we grow in such spiritual power."[10] We have a need to see ourselves reflected in our role models and leaders. I also agree with other Church writers who have discussed the power that comes when women learn doctrine from other women,[11] including talks given in general conference. It is important to see and hear from more women in all settings so our identity can include the attributes we see in these women leaders. We all benefit as we watch, listen, and reflect on gospel concepts and doctrines taught by women (and men).

One scholar, Melissa Inouye, reflected on the importance of identifying with leaders and exemplars. She said, "Observing the difference that the messenger—not just the message—makes in people's ability to be engaged was instructive. When my fellow branch members saw someone with whom they identified (with whom they had something significant in common and who was also known to them through long acquaintance), they were more receptive to the message that was being taught and more engaged in the conference itself. . . . The same is true for the young women and single women that the Church is struggling to retain. To help women within the Church deepen their connection and commitment to the kingdom of God, the kingdom of God needs more women leaders."[12]

When we have a variety of women as role models, we can "see potential paths played out in others' lives before enacting them in our own. . . . When women do not see themselves reflected in the images that represent us as a people, there is for some women a sense of invisibility and thus unimportance."[13] It's hard to be what you can't see. Sheri L. Dew stated, "Confusion about our identity can wreak havoc. But clarity about who we are is empowering."[14] Young women, please understand that it is critical for you

10. Ulrich, *Live Up to Our Privileges*, 128.
11. McBaine, *Women at Church*, 146–147.
12. Ibid., 37.
13. Ibid., 40.
14. Dew, *Women and the Priesthood*, 44, 47.

to envision your unique identity. Seek revelation to help you on this important journey.

One critical role model, in my opinion, should be our Heavenly Mother. The Church of Jesus Christ of Latter-day Saints teaches that "all human beings, male and female, are beloved spirit children of heavenly parents, a Heavenly Father and a Heavenly Mother. This understanding is rooted in scriptural and prophetic teachings about the nature of God, our relationship to Deity, and the godly potential of men and women. The doctrine of a Heavenly Mother is a cherished and distinctive belief among Latter-day Saints."[15] I am thrilled that this doctrine is now discussed more frequently, as I believe it is critical for what is called positive "identity formation and development" in all Young Women and sisters in the Church. Church leaders have taught that "all men and women are in the similitude of the universal Father and Mother and are literally the sons and daughters of Deity."[16] Susa Young Gates, a prominent figure in the Church in the early 1900s, wrote that Joseph Smith's visions and teachings revealed the truth that "the divine Mother, [is] side by side with the divine Father."[17] Finally, Professor Valerie Hudson, who has written extensively on women in the Church, stated: "I am made in the image of my Heavenly Mother, who is a goddess as wise, loving, and powerful as my Heavenly Father."[18]

Now I'm not saying that men cannot be our role models. As our Savior, Christ should always be the most prominent role model in our lives. But girls and women—consciously and unconsciously—will form their core identity by watching and listening to women. As we study, ponder, and pray to understand more about our Heavenly Mother, it can help us envision our future roles, which can include an image of becoming a Goddess ourselves. This is deep, I

---

15. "Mother in Heaven," in *Gospel Topics Essays,* para. 1.
16. The First Presidency of the Church, "The Origin of Man," 78.
17. Gates, "The Vision Beautiful," 542–543.
18. Hudson, "Searching for Heavenly Mother: Why? Why not? How?" para. 13.

know! As the Young Women General Presidency stated in 2020, "A continued focus on divine identity will bring power to each young woman, changing her heart through faith in His name."

IDENTITIES

Christian writer Gordon T. Smith wrote that "we cannot serve with grace and we cannot make a difference for God in the lives of others if we violate who we are."[19] He also taught: "To know ourselves and be true to ourselves is to be true to God. For to be true to ourselves is to be true to how God has made us, how God has crafted our personalities, how God has given us ability and talent. God will call us to serve him in the church and the world; however, this calling will always be consistent with who we are, with whom he created us to be. Know yourself, for you cannot live in truth until and unless you do."[20]

So, who are you? Your identities can include being a daughter of earthly and Heavenly Parents. They can also include roles like sister, niece, aunt, young woman of color, athlete, active Church member, class president, outdoor enthusiast, community volunteer, musician, artist, introvert, friend, social justice advocate, public speaker, gifted listener, New Yorker, native of Denmark, and more. However, with all these potentially good identities, I must briefly discuss one of the most troubling identity trends I have seen in recent years. More and more girls and women are focused on external appearance more than on the internal matters of identity. The image they have of their bodies seems to be taking over their perceived "identity." If your identity has been or is being formed primarily based on what your body looks like, then it will damage your perception of who you truly are. This is definitely at odds with a firm belief that you are a daughter of Heavenly Parents. See chapters 11 and 12 for deeper discussions of social media and body image.

---

19. Smith, *Courage and Calling*, 37.
20. Ibid., 38.

LEADERSHIP IDENTITY

Research tells us that boys are socialized much more often to see themselves as future leaders than girls. In fact, at every age, males are more likely to see leaders who look like them. This means that teen and young adult women often struggle to embrace what is called a leadership identity. Basically, if we can't *envision* ourselves as leaders or at least potential leaders, we don't *aspire* to lead. If we don't aspire to lead, then we don't *prepare* ourselves to lead. For example, if you don't aspire to attend college, you won't do the things you need to do to make sure you are prepared. If you don't plan to get sealed in the temple, you won't do what you need to do to be prepared. The same is true for developing leadership skills. If you don't embrace a leadership identity, you most likely won't intentionally work on developing the skills needed to become a leader. Finding and embracing a leadership identity is very important in your preparation to lead.

To develop a leadership identity, you must integrate three elements. First, you need to see yourself as a leader, which is referred to as claiming. If you don't ever claim you are a leader, then you won't become a leader. I'm not saying you need to claim it out loud. Claiming it internally is a more powerful process anyway. The second element is referred to as granting, which focuses on relationships. Basically, it is when someone you know recognizes and follows you in some way. And the final piece is called endorsement, when a group of people recognizes you (formally or informally) as a leader for a project, event, activity, or movement. It can even include following someone when they take a stand about something—like walking out of an inappropriate movie.

The combination of these three—*claiming, granting*, and *endorsing*—can solidify a leadership identity more firmly than one or two of them. For example, if people are following—granting—but you don't ever internally claim, you will continue to struggle with leadership identity. As you work to implement each of these three concepts, your leadership identity should get stronger and more stable.[21] When a girl or woman sees herself as a leader, her motivation to lead is strengthened, her engagement in the leadership process increases, she will seek out more leadership responsibilities, and she will more consciously look for opportunities to develop leadership skills.

When I was a young woman, I developed and strengthened my leadership identity by teaching piano and violin lessons, taking on leadership roles (both formal and informal) on sports teams, babysitting my five younger brothers, teaching dances to my peers for an upcoming regional dance festival, overseeing the planning of youth events, directing my high school choir when my teacher had to miss class, pulling together groups to sing in sacrament meeting, and working hard to be involved in early morning seminary to set an example for others (a request that came from my father). One of my good friends, however, strengthened her leadership identity through reaching out and listening to others, defusing tense situations with her humor, providing opportunities and transportation for others to do service, working as a supervisor in a store, and being the first follower to efforts I led, which resulted in more followers. All of these examples provided the elements of claiming, granting, and endorsing for both my friend and me. She *granted* and helped *endorse* me, and I did the same for her.

STRATEGIES

You can use many approaches to build and strengthen your leadership identity. Honestly, all the strategies I've provided in chapters 5–9 are important in the development of leadership identity as well. In addition to those, doing the following will help you continue along your journey of preparing to lead:

1. **Study the Lives of Women:** Take the time to read and think about women in the Bible, Book of Mormon, and Church history. Jot down characteristics and qualities you

---

21. DeRue and Ashford, "Who Will Lead and Who Will Follow?"

see in them as you study. Consider how they responded to challenges and opportunities. In addition, read Church teachings about Mother in Heaven.

2. **Observe Faithful Women:** It is also important to observe the leadership qualities and skills of women in your life, including mothers, relatives, Young Women leaders, community leaders, and more. Think about and record the qualities you see in them that you would like to strengthen in yourself.

3. **Explore Your Identities:** Think about the different roles or identities that you have in your life (see "Identities" section for examples) and record them in your journal or the workbook that accompanies this book. Which are most important to you? What does your leadership identity look like? How strong is your identity as a daughter of Heavenly Parents?

4. **Claim, Grant, and Endorse:** Pay attention to how you claim leadership, how others grant and endorse your leadership, and how you grant and endorse others. Being a powerful follower can help you learn leadership too. How do you grant and endorse for others? The process of claiming, granting, and endorsing can happen in all settings, including home, school, church, and community.

CONCLUSION

The most important aspect of your identity is that it must first be anchored in the belief that you are "a beloved daughter of heavenly parents, with a divine nature and eternal destiny."[22] I truly believe that part of your destiny is to become a leader. President Gordon B. Hinckley declared: "You can be a leader. You must be a leader . . . in those causes for which this Church stands. . . . The adversary of all truth would put into your heart a reluctance to make an effort. Cast that fear aside and be valiant in the cause of

---

22. "Young Women Theme," para. 1.

truth and righteousness."[23] You have no idea how many people in your life are waiting for you to lead the way.

I appreciate this statement by Sheri L. Dew: "We will never be happy or feel peace; we will never deal well with life's stresses and ambiguities; we will never live up to who we are as women of God unless we overcome our mortal identity crisis and understand who we have always been and who we may become. The truth about who we are and who we have always been carries a sense of purpose that cannot be duplicated in any other way."[24]

Seek to see yourself through God's eyes, and that will make all the difference.

---

23. Hinckley, "Stand Up for Truth," 5–6.
24. Dew, *Women and the Priesthood*, 44.

PART III

Challenges

CHAPTER 11
Social Media

"Use your voice and your power to articulate what you know and feel—on social media, in quiet conversations with your friends, when you're chatting with your grandchildren. Tell them why you believe, what it feels like, if you ever doubted, how you got through it, and what Jesus Christ means to you."[1]

—SHARON EUBANK

Part III of this book provides content that will help you think about some of the complex challenges you most likely have or will face along your leadership preparation journey. These are very real trials that nearly all of you grapple with either personally or as you interact with friends who struggle. This section of the book begins with this chapter discussing social media, followed by chapters exploring body image and mental health struggles. These three chapters will be intertwined in many ways. Finally, the fourth and last chapter in this section will grapple with mixed messages you may encounter in the Church.

In today's world, social media impacts nearly everyone's life in some way. It can definitely be a positive influence. For example, Elder Gary E. Stevenson of the Quorum of the Twelve Apostles has spoken multiple times about how social media can spread "the knowledge

---

1. Eubank, "Turn on Your Light," 7.

of a Savior . . . throughout every nation, kindred, tongue, and people."[2] He stated that various platforms "have generated hundreds of millions of likes, shares, views, retweets, and pins and have become very effective and efficient in sharing the gospel with family, friends, and associates."[3] However, there are many downsides to social media.

This chapter will focus on how social media, if we are not careful, can negatively impact our progress toward preparing to lead. If social media is not used wisely, it can halt our development and negatively impact our confidence, mindsets, purpose and callings, identity, and perceptions of our gifts, talents and strengths—everything we have been talking about in part II of this book. I'm going to be real here and not pull punches. I believe that the more you know, the more you are empowered to make intentional choices.

SETTING THE STAGE

According to a 2015 study published in the *Journal of Medical Internet Research*, more than 95 percent of young adults and adolescents had an online presence.[4] And in a 2018 Pew Research Center survey, researchers found that 45 percent of teens at that time were online almost constantly and 97 percent had at least one social media platform (Instagram, Snapchat, Facebook, and YouTube).[5] Another 2018 survey[6] showed that, on average, teens are online almost nine hours a day, not including time for homework. Honestly, I expect those percentages are now even higher. Social media use is everywhere. Although social media technologies provide a great way to engage and communicate, these platforms are associated with intense pressures and risks.

As we all know, social media impacts the way we feel about ourselves, and studies have shown that the "more time people spend on social media, the more likely they are to be lonely."[7] This is just one

---

2. Stevenson, "Spiritual Eclipse," 46.
3. Ibid.
4. Yonker, Zan, Scirica, Jethwani, and Kinane, "'Friending' Teens: Systematic Review of Social Media in Adolescent and Young Adult Health Care."
5. Mayo Clinic, "Teens and Social Media Use: What's the Impact?"
6. "Social Media and Teens," American Academy of Child & Adolescent Psychiatry.
7. "Viewpoint: Use Social Media Wisely," *Church News*, para. 7.

of the numerous downsides of social media, which can in turn negatively impact our learning and development. Bonnie L. Oscarson, former Young Women General President, said: "If we are not vigilant in how we use our personal devices, we too can begin to turn inward and forget that the essence of living the gospel is service."[8] Though challenging, we must have a healthy approach and respect for social media and its consequences.

Teenage years and young adulthood are times when we are most vulnerable to mental health risks. The research on the impacts of social media on mental health helps us see the risks more clearly and helps us understand the negative, though sometimes subtle, impact social media can have on us. For example, in 2018, a UK study explored whether social media use during teenage years was associated with depression, harassment, self-esteem, and body image. The research team studied more than 10,000 fourteen-year-olds and found that when girls increased their social media use—three to five hours a day—they had more depression, poor sleep, low self-esteem, and poor body image. If they were on social media even more than this, girls experienced still higher rates of body weight dissatisfaction, higher depressive symptoms, and an even greater loss of self-esteem.[9]

PRESSURES

There is so much pressure for girls to conform to social standards for approval and acceptance ("likes") online. Unsurprisingly, studies show that girls and young women are now less satisfied with their bodies and notice their "perceived" flaws in greater detail than in past decades.[10] This cycle of pressure and critique is a lose-lose situation for a girl's self-esteem. And when you combine these pressures with cyberbullying, more young women have increased isolation, hopelessness, depression, and anxiety.[11]

---

8. Oscarson, "The Needs Before Us," 25.
9. Kelly, Zilanawala, Booker, and Sacker, "Social Media Use and Adolescent Mental Health."
10. Ibid.
11. Luxton, June, and Fairall, "Social Media and Suicide: A Public Health Perspective."

Studies also show that girls are now posting more and more provocative photos of themselves on social media. In fact, young women are much more likely to post pictures of themselves wearing revealing clothes—to show how they look—than young men.[12] It seems there are more pressures for girls to post sexually expressive photos. If you are on social media a lot, you'll see influencers, celebrities, or popular teens share these types of photos—often airbrushed images—and, whether or not you know it, you subtly internalize the messages you see. Research says that you often begin to feel that your own online photos represent who you really are, and you may judge yourselves harshly. Additionally, you are critiqued by others more often because the photos are online.

Without social media, young women in the past—like me—might have used diaries or journals to record our ideas, thoughts, and experiences. And occasionally we may have cautiously shared them with a close friend. However, now, with social media, kids and teens are more likely to share private thoughts on public platforms. This could be great in some ways, but it also creates new pressures and challenges that can more easily impact one's sense of self-worth. Teenage and young adult years are exciting but also a tough time for most people. This was true even before social media! Figuring out who you are, developing a sense of self, wrestling with body image, and learning how to relate to others are just a few of the crazy dynamics you probably face every day.

DANGERS

Even though I didn't plan to share a lot of research in this book, I just cannot help myself. I'm a researcher through and through, so hang in there because this is really important. A compelling 2015 study was conducted in Italy using Twitter.[13] One particularly dangerous social media trend was a Twitter movement called Proana, which is a group

---

12. Yonker, Zan, Scirica, Jethwani, and Kinane, "'Friending' Teens: Systematic Review of Social Media in Adolescent and Young Adult Health Care."
13. Bert, Gualano, Camussi, and Siliquini, "Risks and Threats of Social Media Websites: Twitter and the Proana Movement."

of followers who consider themselves to be pro-anorexia. Yes, you heard that correctly. Imagine advocating for a dangerous eating disorder where people place such a high value on controlling their weight and shape that they take extreme efforts to keep an abnormally low body weight that drastically interferes with their lives![14] This team of academics used Twitter Search to retrieve the Proana accounts and analyzed the group's number of followers, tweets, and other biographical information. The results were stunning: they retrieved 341 accounts, and 97.9% of the followers were teenage girls. Week after week, they found an increase in both followers and tweets using hashtags like #thinspiration, #anatips, and #fastingcompetition.

While Proana is only one group focused on anorexia on Twitter, I'm sure the negative impact on many lives was and still is devastating. And I assume that there are many other groups like this out there that want to pull girls and women in. As doctors and researchers continue to study and understand the power social media has over its users, they are getting a much clearer picture of how social media sites are targeting vulnerabilities of teenage and college-aged women.[15] Unfortunately, this gives young women like you a dangerous incentive to think poorly of yourselves and puts you at increased risk for many negative outcomes. As you know, social media's influence can feel overpowering.

Interestingly, research also tells us that boys seem to be impacted less by social media than girls and more by video games (though video games sometimes function as their own type of social media when played online in a group). Boys and girls use social media for some of the same reasons—to connect with friends, see what everyone is doing, or share what they're doing. Boys tend to use social media with more of a "third person" approach.[16] They will show the basketball game they're attending, a trophy they won, a car they like, or a group of their friends. Their posts are generally about

---

14. Mayo Clinic, "Anorexia Nervosa."
15. Ibid.
16. Kelly, Zilanawala, Booker, and Sacker, "Social Media Use and Adolescent Mental Health."

what they're doing. Girls tend to use social media as more of a "first person" approach. They post pictures of themselves alone and with girlfriends. Their faces are generally in every picture, and their posts are generally about their lives.[17]

Young women can get preoccupied with spending more time and effort creating "just" the right image to post on social media, often relying on filters to create an illusion of perfection. And, as trends like the "Proana" movement show us, this preoccupation can be a trap leading down a negative self-esteem spiral filled with judgment and shame. Those unrealistic or airbrushed images posted by celebrities or influencers don't help at all. If you are on social media a lot, you cannot help but compare.

COMPARISONS

Much of the chapter has already talked about the tendency to compare yourself to others, which is actually an age-old problem. In fact, Eleanor Roosevelt, an American political figure, diplomat, and activist, was attributed with saying this in 1931: "Great minds discuss ideas; Average minds discuss events; Small minds discuss people."[18] Gossiping and talking about others is most definitely a form of comparison.

Everybody's life has both happy times and sad times, and what is shown on social media is only a slice of someone's experience. Plus, at that, what is posted on social media is typically only the best stuff—only what people want you to see. In fact, many images on social media are not real at all. President M. Russell Ballard of the Quorum of the Twelve Apostles said: "We live in a world of comparison. Social media has made this worse as we go online and compare our seemingly less exciting lives with the 'fake lives' we see online. Many of those fake lives are edited, boastful, and unreal. Some people may have unrealistic expectations that they should be happy all the time, and if they are not, they feel like something is

---

17. Ibid.
18. Roosevelt, Eleanor, "Eleanor Roosevelt Quotes."

wrong with them. We should not compare ourselves with others."[19] Yet, I will totally admit, it is much harder than it sounds. Popular Church speaker and author John Hilton III wrote: "Comparison is the thief of joy . . . and looks at what is or isn't and wishes that it were something else."[20] Peace, he said, comes when you "look at what is or isn't" and are grateful for all of it.[21]

STRATEGIES

So, how can you work with yourself to decrease the negative effects of social media in your life? I offer four strategies:

1. **Set Reasonable Limits:** Reflect on how you can avoid letting social media interfere with important activities in your life (like sleep, meals, homework, and time with family and friends). Social media fasts can also help you create boundaries that you may want to put on social media in your everyday life.

2. **Ask Yourself Questions:** When I am on social media, do I feel better or worse about myself? How would others I love feel about themselves if they saw this post? When I am posting, what feelings do I experience? What are the reasons behind the messages people are posting?

3. **Conduct an Audit:** Go through your social media posts from the last week or so (on platforms where this is possible) and do a personal audit. Are you spreading rumors, bullying or damaging another's reputation, posting provocative pictures of yourself, or doing anything you would be embarrassed to show to a responsible parent or guardian? Are you posting things that will make others feel excluded? If so, make plans to do better. Also pay attention to how much time you are spending on social media throughout your day.

4. **Focus More Time on Meaningful Activities:** Ensure you are taking time for meaningful activities in your life, including

---

19. Ballard, "Questions and Answers," para. 19.
20. Hilton, *The Founder of Our Peace*, 33–34.
21. Ibid., 36.

efforts to learn and grow. The chapters in part II provide many ideas of things you can do to strengthen your influence and leadership abilities. In addition, developing deeper and better relationships—particularly face-to-face—with your parents, siblings, relatives, and friends can teach you so many things about life and leadership.

CONCLUSION

I will conclude with a quote from Drs. Lexi and Lindsey Kite's book, *More Than a Body,* that provides some wonderful advice: "Once you unfollow, unsubscribe, mute, and opt out of those media choices that send you on dangerous, expensive, unfulfilling excursions, you've got a lot more room on your map and time in your day to chart a new course. What do you want to learn or experience? What accounts, shows, books, podcasts, pages, websites, music, and people do you want to listen to? What messages help remind you of your worth and power beyond your body? What inspires you to be more? What expands your vision, your hope, your knowledge and skills? What lights you up and motivates you? As you actively seek out media that inspires you to be more . . . [it] will reveal new ways of living, doing, and being that lead to even more fulfilling destinations."[22]

Although social media can be used as a force for good in staying connected with friends and family, sharing talents, finding community and support for specific activities, preaching the gospel, and serving the Lord, it must be used with care, compassion, and caution. If we are preparing for a "future greater than anything [we] can imagine,"[23] we must use our time and emotional energy to concentrate on things that empower us and others to learn, grow, develop, and serve. Although this journey is one that is often less traveled, it is truly the voyage that will bring us more joy. The choice is yours.

---

22. Kite and Kite, *More Than a Body: Your Body is an Instrument, Not an Ornament,* 90.
23. Uchtdorf, "Living the Gospel Joyful," 121.

CHAPTER 12

Body Image

"We see women, including ourselves, as bodies first and people second. . . . We are all at a severe disadvantage when our self-perceptions and body images are so deeply tied to how we look (or how we think we look). Too many of us not only feel awful about our looks, since we can never achieve or maintain the aspirational beauty ideals presented to us, but also feel awful about our dynamic, adaptive, miraculous bodies overall because all we care about is how they look. This is truly the root of negative body image."[1]

—DRS. LEXIE AND LINDSAY KITE,
AUTHORS OF *MORE THAN A BODY*

Struggles around body image are rampant for girls and women today. Honestly, this topic is one of my greatest concerns for young women in the Church right now, because it is at the heart of many other downward patterns that I have seen sisters fall prey to. We can tell you all day long that it is "what's inside that really matters," and I expect you are told this often by your loved ones. But it is

---

1. Kite and Kite, *More Than a Body: Your Body is an Instrument, Not an Ornament*, 6.

difficult to not be consumed with appearance in the world today. I get it. However, if you let yourselves be pulled in by those constant messages—and they are everywhere—I fear that your progress toward learning, growing, and developing leadership qualities will be delayed or even halted.

Church leaders have addressed this topic on occasion. For example, a 2019 *Ensign* article stated, "Our nurturing Heavenly Father has two eyes, two hands, two feet, and one heart—just like us. We are made after the image of God, even if details of our shape, size, and color may differ. We should celebrate those details! We may never feel as though we fit societal ideals of beauty, but what is more beautiful than the self-assurance that comes from this simple truth: 'I am a child of God'?"[2] Susan W. Tanner, former Young Women General President, also taught that "happiness comes from accepting the bodies we have been given as divine gifts and enhancing our natural attributes, not from remaking our bodies after the image of the world. The Lord wants us to be made over—but in His image, not in the image of the world, by receiving His image in our countenances."[3]

You have been taught these principles for years but, for many of you, they are often hard to put into practice. In this chapter, I don't attempt to cover all of the important elements that can be included in a complete discussion on body image. However, there are a few areas that I feel guided to include. First, I set the stage overall and then discuss the "fixing culture" and influences, followed by several "body image resilience"[4] strategies.

SETTING THE STAGE

Body image is "the perception that a person has of their physical self and the thoughts and feelings that result from that perception.

2. DeTavis, "Rethinking Beauty: A Gospel Perspective on Body Image," 78.
3. Tanner, "The Sanctity of the Body," 14–15.
4. Kite and Kite, *More Than a Body: Your Body is an Instrument, Not an Ornament.*

These feelings can be positive, negative, or both and are influenced by individual and environmental factors."[5] Researchers have found that numerous considerations (such as media, family, and peers) cause women to internalize societal beauty ideals that can lead to satisfaction or dissatisfaction with their bodies. As discussed in the last chapter, the influence of social media has now become one of the key driving forces of negative body image perceptions among young women.

A negative body image can hold girls and women back in numerous ways, and unfortunately, many suffer with this for their whole lives. At the root of negative body image is what is called self-objectification, which is a person seeing themselves as an object for use rather than a human being. According to body image experts Drs. Lindsey and Lexie Kite, self-objectification puts "all the focus on how our bodies look rather than how we feel or what we can do," and it "prevents us from seeing ourselves as God sees us: as children of our Heavenly Parents with inherent, unchangeable value."[6] In their book, *More than a Body*, one of the authors exclaimed: "My body was never the problem; my perception of my body was the problem."[7] Unfortunately, we also see this when girls are taught that it is their job to make sure the boys and men around them do not have impure thoughts. This reinforces the idea that you are an object, that how you look is your central identity.

Some teen and young adult women don't believe that self-objectification is a big deal, but it is incredibly distracting, disrupting, and damaging. It can prevent us from being fully engaged in our lives, whether in school, church, extracurricular activities, or social and personal relationships. It can also prevent us from discovering and utilizing our gifts and talents. In short, it can keep us from becoming the women our Heavenly Parents want and need us to be. The emotional

---

5. "What is Body Image?" National Eating Disorders Collaboration, 1.
6. Kite and Kite, "More Than a Body: Seeing as God Sees," 10.
7. Kite and Kite, *More Than a Body: Your Body is an Instrument, Not an Ornament,* 35.

work involved in self-objectification takes energy that can deplete joy and fulfillment in our activities and lives.[8] In fact, according to Drs. Kite, "Constant attention to physical appearance saps your mental and physical energy, making it nearly impossible to reach or maintain a flow state."[9]

THE "FIXING" CULTURE

We live in a culture where there is pressure to "fix ourselves" as women in different ways. In no arena is this more true, however, than in the pressure to fix our appearance. We believe that if we look better (whatever that means to us), then we will feel better about ourselves. But, as Drs. Kite explained, "The truth is, being defined by our appearance is the real problem, and the endless beauty work we do to improve our confidence and body image is just a symptom of the problem, not the solution."[10]

Research shows that poor body image affects girls and women worldwide. In fact, over a decade ago, researchers found that approximately 80 percent of US women do not like how they look, 70 percent of women in a healthy weight range want to be thinner, and 81 percent of ten-year-olds are already afraid of being fat.[11] Further, 53 percent of thirteen-year-old American girls are unhappy with their bodies, and the percentage grows to 78 percent by the time girls reach seventeen. Sadly, more than 50 percent of teen girls use unhealthy weight control behaviors such as skipping meals, vomiting, taking laxatives, and fasting. I expect these statistics have dramatically increased in the past decade.[12]

In 2020, The Women and Equalities Committee of the UK House of Commons conducted a survey about body image. Out

---

8. Ibid., 105.
9. Ibid.
10. Ibid., 115.
11. Gallivan, "Teens, Social Media and Body Image"; "Statistics," Center of Excellence for Eating Disorders; "Eating Disorder Statistics," National Association of Anorexia Nervosa and Associated Disorders.
12. Ibid.

of the 7,878 participants (including women, men, transgender, and non-binary individuals of all ages), 61 percent of adults and 66 percent of children felt "negative" or "very negative" about their body image most of the time; about 62 percent of women felt negatively about their bodies, compared to 53 percent of men;[13] 85 percent of participants under the age of eighteen thought their appearance was "very important" or "important"; 86 percent of adults said their mental health was impacted by the way they felt about their body; and participants under the age of eighteen reported that social media had the greatest influence on their body image. When asked how they would consider altering their appearance, 8 in 10 young people said they would use diet and exercise, half would use weight-loss products, and 3 in 10 would use shapewear, non-surgical cosmetic treatments, and cosmetic surgery.[14]

A few years ago, my team and I explored the research around body image and cosmetic surgery in the state of Utah. As you may know, more than half of the state's residents are members of the Church, so it is an interesting case to consider even if you don't live in Utah or even in the US. We found that Utah women's close attention to personal appearance manifested in various ways. *Forbes* magazine reported that in 2006 Salt Lake City residents spent $2.2 million on hair coloring and $6.9 million on cosmetics and skin-care products—more than ten times the amount residents of similarly sized cities spent.[15] Utah is in the Mountain/Pacific region, which has the nation's highest rates of cosmetic procedures, and the most popular procedure in the region is breast augmentation.[16] The most common Google search for plastic surgery in Utah was "breast implants."[17] In addition, a qualitative

13. House of Commons Women and Equalities Committee, "Changing the Perfect Picture: An Inquiry into Body Image: Sixth Report of Session 2019–21."
14. House of Commons Women and Equalities Committee, "Body Image Survey Results: First Special Report of Session 2019–21."
15. Ruiz, "America's Vainest Cities."
16. "2015 Plastic Surgery Statistics Report." American Society of Plastic Surgeons.
17. "Most Searched Plastic Surgery Procedures by State." Plastic Surgery Portal.

research study on Latter-day Saint women in Utah showed that breast augmentations are sometimes given to young women as a high school graduation gift from their parents.[18]

According to the American Society for Aesthetic Plastic Surgery, in 2016 Americans spent a record setting 13.5 billion dollars on aesthetic procedures (surgical and nonsurgical combined).[19] Between the years of 2000 and 2015, the total number of cosmetic procedures performed in the United States increased by 115 percent.[20] The large increase in procedures deemed "minimally invasive" was so high that it led to the overall dramatic increase in total procedures. In fact, minimally invasive cosmetic procedures have become increasingly common for those who want to improve their appearance. In the US, dermatologists report that Botox injections have become almost as great a part of their business as skin cancer treatments.

Overall, research shows that body image plays a part in the decision to undergo elective plastic surgery and other body altering procedures. Kathy Davis, a leading scholar in this field, says, "Cosmetic surgery belongs to a broad regime of technologies, practices and discourses which define the female body as deficient and in need of constant transformation."[21] As my peers and I reported, women who received high scores on a scale of body shame and self-surveillance were more likely to express positive feelings about plastic surgery and to report a likelihood that they would modify their own bodies in the future.[22] Despite the definite connection between poor body image and strong societal pressures on girls and women to conform to impossible standards of physical beauty, some people see

---

18. Namie, "'In the World, But Not of the World'."
19. "American Society for Aesthetic Plastic Surgery Reports More Than $13.5 Billion Spent for the First Time Ever." American Society for Aesthetic Plastic Surgery.
20. "2015 Plastic Surgery Statistics Report." American Society of Plastic Surgeons.
21. Madsen, Dillon, & Scribner, "Cosmetic Surgery and Body Image among Utah Women," 1.
22. Ibid.

no problem with plastic surgery and even encourage it. And some feel that efforts to improve their physical appearance (no matter how extreme) are justified. But I want to caution you about this. If we expend a significant portion of our time and energy on altering our exteriors, we will miss many opportunities to improve and grow in areas of deeper importance and longer lasting value. Some women believe that physically modifying their bodies will boost their confidence and solve all their problems. It will not. Strengthening your identity as a daughter of Heavenly Parents is the answer.

INFLUENCES

Although body image concerns are widespread during the teen years, many researchers have found that those concerns are influenced much earlier in girls' upbringings. In fact, some studies have found body dissatisfaction can be found in children at the age of five, and these concerns continue to grow through young adulthood.[23] Young girls become aware that how they look is very important when they are praised, rewarded, and valued for their beauty. We often do this naturally to be kind, and honestly sometimes little girls are so cute. It is even hard for me as a grandmother not to constantly talk about how cute my granddaughter is. However, I don't want my granddaughter to grow up thinking that her appearance is what makes her valuable and powerful.[24] This is a trap. Of course, the influence of parents is the strongest relationship that girls have during preteen years, so their mother's influence is front and center. One set of researchers found that if mothers have a preoccupation with their own weight and shape and are self-critical, their daughters may also grow up placing great value on the importance of being thin and will regularly criticize themselves.[25] If

---

23. Craddock, Diedrichs, Slater, Gentili, Thornton, Smith, and Garbett, "Written Evidence Submitted by the Centre for Appearance Research."
24. Kite and Kite, *More Than a Body: Your Body is an Instrument, Not an Ornament*, 317.
25. Handford, Rapee, and Fardouly, "The Influence of Maternal Modeling on Body Image Concerns and Eating Disturbances in Preadolescent Girls."

mothers and other female influencers demonstrate positive healthy behaviors (such as regular exercise and healthy eating), daughters will follow suit. Be aware of the subtle unhelpful messages you may be receiving from other important people in your life too.

As discussed in the last chapter, social media can deeply impact a young woman's body image, as can television, movies, videos, and frankly all kinds of media and other sources of information. Basically, "we grow up seeing idealized and sexualized female bodies presented in media as parts for others' viewing pleasure."[26] "We learn that the most important thing about women is their bodies, and the most important thing about women's bodies is how they look."[27] This is a lie. Just being aware of these influences is a start.

Finally, some of the strongest negative influences on body image come from messages you receive about food. Dieting in general can lead to a lifetime of difficulty with food. Researchers conducted a large study of fourteen- and fifteen-year-olds and found that dieting was the most important predictor of developing an eating disorder. In fact, "those who dieted moderately were five times more likely to develop an eating disorder and those who practiced extreme restriction were eighteen times more likely to develop an eating disorder than those who did not diet."[28] Listen to the messages of validation and love from your Heavenly Parents who have blessed you with a body that may not seem perfect, but is perfectly capable of so many amazing things. Embrace your body and use it for good!

STRATEGIES

I have known Drs. Lexie and Lindsay Kite, authors of *More Than a Body*, for many years. I respect them and their work, which is based on extensive research. I've cited them heavily in this chapter,

---

26. Kite and Kite, *More Than a Body: Your Body is an Instrument, Not an Ornament*, 2–3.
27. Ibid., 3.
28. Ibid., 214.

and I'll offer strategies and advice directly from their work as well. They focus on how to strengthen what they call "body image resilience" and believe that when you cultivate this resilience, you can connect or reconnect with your "life's power, purpose, and possibilities outside the framework of looking or feeling beautiful."[29] Here are some strategies they suggest:

1. **Try a Media Fast or Cleanse:** Choose a time period (like three days, a week, a month, or whatever makes sense for you) and avoid media as much as possible. This includes TV, movies, magazines, or use any social media apps like Instagram, Twitter, Snapchat, TikTok, or Facebook. This can also include some books, music, and podcasts as well because they can also be filled with "objectifying body ideals."[30] Of course, you will need to use your own judgment on what this looks like based on how various media impact thoughts about your body.

2. **Ask Yourself These Questions:** How much or how often do I think about my appearance? How much energy and money are focused on my looks? Does it feel appropriate? Why do I spend this much energy and money on my appearance? Could my time, money, and other resources be used in better ways? What benefits do I receive from the resources I expend on my beauty? How is my body a gift?

3. **Become More Self-Compassionate:** Rather than criticizing yourself for your appearance, the way you feel about it, or your actions related to appearance, try taking a deep breath and feel self-compassion. To do this, you can speak kindly to yourself and acknowledge the pain, confusion, and pressure you feel about your body.[31] Then affirm—within your mind and heart—that you are okay and doing your best. Breathe. Beating yourself up is not the answer.

---

29. Ibid., 31.
30. Kite and Kite, *More Than a Body: Your Body is an Instrument, Not an Ornament.*
31. Ibid., 142–143.

4. **Help Others:** You can help others by complimenting them on non-appearance-related characteristics and talents, which will in turn help you focus your thoughts away from appearance. For example, you could tell others what you have observed about their character, interactions, talents, behaviors, admirable qualities, and more.

CONCLUSION

According to Drs. Kite, "Positive body image isn't believing your body looks good; it is knowing your body is good, regardless of how it looks."[32] Having a body is a blessing from the Lord. When we accept and respect our bodies, we can do more. As these authors say often, let's see our bodies as instruments and not ornaments. Elder Jeffrey R. Holland of the Quorum of the Twelve Apostles once stated: "I plead with you young women to please be more accepting of yourselves, including your body shape and style, with a little less longing to look like someone else. We are all different. Some are tall, and some are short. Some are round, and some are thin. And almost everyone at some time or other wants to be something they are not! . . . Every young woman is a child of destiny and every adult woman a powerful force for good."[33]

Although it is difficult to not be consumed with appearance in the world today, you can take responsibility for your own thoughts and actions, no matter what others say and do. You are a daughter of Heavenly Parents, and your body is a gift. Use this incredible gift, instead of being used by it, to further your work and goals toward seeing and preparing for that future only God can see for you. Don't let body image challenges take away from your preparation to lead.

---

32. Kite and Kite, *More Than a Body: Your Body is an Instrument, Not an Ornament.*
33. Holland, "To Young Women," 29.

CHAPTER 13
Mental Health

"How do you best respond when mental or
emotional challenges confront you or those you love?
Above all, never lose faith in your Father in Heaven,
who loves you more than you can comprehend. . . .
Never, ever doubt that, and never harden your heart.
Faithfully pursue the time-tested devotional practices
that bring the Spirit of the Lord into your life . . .
[and] hold fast to the perfecting promises of the
Atonement of Jesus Christ."

—ELDER JEFFREY R. HOLLAND[1]

This section of the book is about what I believe are key challenges
teen and young adult women face today, and mental health is one
that many experts[2] would agree is of great concern. In fact, my guess
is that every young woman will either struggle with one or more
mental health concerns or will certainly know a loved one who does.
Either way, it could impact your growth, learning, and development,
which can affect your leadership. Although things are changing,

---

1. Holland, "Like a Broken Vessel," 40–41.
2. Desilver, "The Concerns and Challenges of Being a U.S. Teen."; "Adolescent
   and Young Adult Health," World Health Organization,

there is still a stigma surrounding topics like depression, anxiety, and suicide, which makes it difficult to have important conversations with family members, friends and peers, and Young Women or Young Adults leaders. But I do hope more of these conversations are occurring in your own settings and circles. Being willing to start a hard conversation and be vulnerable sets a powerful example.

If you struggle yourself, please know you are not alone. BYU religion professor John Hilton III stated, "We all need healing. We may have broken bodies and spirits, or we may have loved ones who do. There is comfort in knowing that the Savior can mend all wounds."[3] If you know others who are struggling, there are ways you can help. Rayna I. Aburto, a member of the General Relief Society Presidency, said, "As disciples of Jesus Christ, we have made a covenant with God that we 'are willing to bear one another's burdens' and 'to mourn with those that mourn.' This may include becoming informed about emotional illnesses, finding resources that can help address these struggles, and ultimately bringing ourselves and others to Christ, who is the Master Healer."[4]

For many teen and young adult women, mental health concerns for self and loved ones could impact so many of the things we have discussed throughout the book thus far (such as the belief that God needs women to lead, levels of confidence, insights about calling and purpose, decisions about attending and finishing college, concerns about body image, and more). This chapter begins with a description of mental health and the top concerns for young women today, followed by a variety of strategies that can help us—and those we can positively influence—improve our mental and emotional health.

DESCRIPTION

According to the World Health Organization (WHO), mental health is defined as "a state of well-being in which the individual realizes his or her own abilities, can cope with the normal stresses

---

3. Hilton, *The Founder of Our Peace*, 111.
4. Aburto, "Thru Cloud and Sunshine, Lord, Abide with Me!" 58.

of life, can work productively, and is able to make a contribution to his or her community."[5] It can include an individual's ability to "enjoy life and to create a balance between life activities and efforts to achieve psychological resilience."[6] According to MentalHealth.gov, "Mental health includes our emotional, psychological, and social well-being. It affects how we think, feel, and act. It also helps determine how we handle stress, relate to others, and make choices."[7] Overall, when you are experiencing positive mental health, you are typically more able to cope with the stresses of life, be more productive with your homework and work, realize your full potential, have increased life satisfaction, make meaningful contributions to people and communities around you,[8] and better prepare to become a leader.

At any age, mental health struggles can impact your thinking, mood, and behavior. Many factors contribute to mental health difficulties, including biological (such as genes or brain chemistry), life experiences (such as trauma or abuse), and a family history of mental health problems. Poor mental health can also be connected to or intensified by several factors, including poverty, lower education levels, poor physical health, and negative life experiences. Mental health conditions can also be compounded by significant physical health problems like diabetes, heart disease, and cancer.[9] Negative life experiences in the home (such as divorce, domestic violence, household substance abuse, and childhood physical or sexual assault) also impact one's mental health.[10] Overall, one report stated that in 2019, nearly 1 in 5 adults in the US (about 20.6 percent) suffered from mental illness and that about 5.2 percent of all adults had a serious mental illness.[11] Although poor mental health is a concern

---

5. "Mental Health: Strengthening Our Response," World Health Organization, 3.
6. Snyder, Lopez, Pedrotti, & Teramoto, *Positive Psychology: The Scientific and Practical Explorations of Human Strengths.*
7. "What is Mental Health?" MentalHealth.gov, para. 1.
8. Ibid.
9. Office of Disease Prevention and Health Promotion. "Mental Health."
10. "Averse Childhood Experiences." Centers for Disease Control and Prevention.
11. "Mental Illness." National Institute of Mental Health.

for people of all ages and can vary by race and ethnicity, women in the US are diagnosed with depression at much higher rates than men.[12]

Struggling with anxiety, depression, or other emotional or behavioral challenges does not mean one isn't cut out to be a leader. As you know by now, I believe that all young women can prepare to influence and lead. Often, the hardships we endure—including mental health challenges—sculpt us into even more resilient, empathetic, and authentic leaders. As Rayna I. Aburto said, "Your struggles do not define you, but they can refine you. Because of a 'thorn in the flesh,' you may have the ability to feel more compassion toward others."[13]

TOP CONCERNS

Sister Aburto explains so well the difference between normal human emotions and mental health concerns: "My dear sisters, it is normal to feel sad or worried once in a while. Sadness and anxiety are natural human emotions. However, if we are constantly sad and if our pain blocks our ability to feel the love of our Heavenly Father and His Son and the influence of the Holy Ghost, then we may be suffering from depression, anxiety, or another emotional condition."[14]

As we educate ourselves on these emotional and mental conditions, we can more quickly recognize when we need help or when people around us may be struggling. If we can quickly acknowledge that something may be "off," then we will be able to get the help we need to feel better again soon. Here are some of the most common mental health issues teen and young adult women face:

---

12. "Complete Health Indicator Report of Depression: Adult Prevalence." Utah Department of Health.
13. Aburto, "Thru Cloud and Sunshine, Lord, Abide with Me!" 59.
14. Ibid.

Depression

Depression is one of the leading causes of illness and disability among teens and young adults.[15] It is a "mood disorder that causes a persistent feeling of sadness and loss of interest. . . . It affects how you feel, think and behave and can lead to a variety of emotional and physical problems. You may have trouble doing normal day-to-day activities, and sometimes you may feel as if life isn't worth living."[16]

Anxiety

Anxiety disorders are the most common mental illnesses, affecting up to 40 percent of women in the course of their lifetimes.[17] According to Harvard Health Publishing, "Adolescent girls are at particularly high risk for the development of anxiety disorders, due to differences in their brain chemistry, psychosocial contributors such as childhood sexual abuse, as well as the hormonal effects of estrogen and progesterone."[18] Google searches for "anxiety" have increased by more than 50 percent over the past five years.[19]

Substance Use Disorder

Substance use disorders are mental disorders that affect people's brains and behaviors. The Center on Addiction has conducted national surveys of teens for over twenty-five years to help document adolescent behavior related to tobacco, alcohol, and other drugs, and have found that even experimenting with any of these can be dangerous. For example, according to research, young people who start drinking before the age of fifteen are four times more likely to develop alcohol dependence later in life.[20]

---

15. "Adolescent Mental Health." World Health Organization.
16. Mayo Clinic. "Depression (Major Depressive Disorder)," para. 1.
17. Collier, "Should We Screen All Adolescent Girls and Women for Anxiety?"
18. Ibid.
19. Hilton, *The Founder of Our Peace*, 2.
20. McCambridge, McAlaney, and Rowe, "Adult Consequences of Late Adolescent Alcohol Consumption."

Eating Disorder

Eating disorders commonly emerge during adolescence and young adulthood, and they affect females more commonly than males.[21] Conditions such as anorexia nervosa, bulimia nervosa, and binge eating disorder are harmful eating behaviors. As I'm sure you know already, "eating disorders are detrimental to health and often co-exist with depression, anxiety and/or substance misuse."[22]

Suicide and Suicidal Ideation

Suicide is the third leading cause of death in fifteen- to nineteen-year-olds around the world[23] and is the second leading cause of death among individuals between ten and thirty-four years of age in the US.[24] While the death rates are staggering, another issue to consider is suicidal ideation, in which an individual seriously thinks about suicide. While 45,000 people died by suicide in the US in 2016, an additional 1.3 million attempted suicide, 2.8 million made a plan, and 9.8 million seriously considered suicide.[25] Suicide attempts and suicidal ideations can also have longterm effects on one's life.

Although various types of mental health challenges can have different warnings signs, one or more of the following feelings or behaviors can help you recognize a problem: having low or no energy, pulling away from people and usual activities, sleeping too much or too little, feeling helpless or hopeless, getting upset or fighting more often with family and friends, inability to perform normal daily tasks, thinking of harming yourself or others, experiencing severe mood swings, feeling unusually confused and forgetful, feeling numb or like nothing matters, eating too much or too little, having unexplained aches and pains, and becoming unusually worried or scared. Many of these elements come with normal life from

---

21. "Adolescent Mental Health." World Health Organization.
22. Ibid.
23. "Adolescent Mental Health." World Health Organization.
24. "Suicide." National Institute of Mental Health.
25. "Preventing Suicide." National Center for Injury Prevention and Control.

time to time and may not be a sign of a mental health struggle, but they can also be warnings signs.

STRATEGIES

Elder Jeffrey R. Holland of the Quorum of the Twelve Apostles gave a groundbreaking general conference talk on mental health in 2013. Not only was he willing to bring up a difficult topic, but he also openly shared some of his own struggles with mental health. In addition, he made a number of recommendations that he believed would help: never lose faith in your Father in Heaven, never harden your heart, faithfully pursue the "time-tested devotional practices that bring the Spirit of the Lord into your life," "seek the counsel of those who hold keys for your spiritual well-being," ask for and cherish priesthood blessings, take the sacrament every week, hold fast to the perfecting promises of the Atonement of Jesus Christ, and believe in miracles.[26] He then continued, "If things continue to be debilitating, seek the advice of reputable people with certified training, professional skills, and good values. Be honest with them about your history and your struggles. Prayerfully and responsibly consider the counsel they give and the solutions they prescribe. . . . Our Father in Heaven expects us to use all of the marvelous gifts He has provided in this glorious dispensation."[27] The best leaders lead by example, and in speaking up about depression, Elder Holland demonstrated his leadership through honesty, faithfulness, and vulnerability.

When it comes to tough topics like suicide, many of us are afraid that in talking about these issues we run the risk of increasing the behavior. A recent *Wall Street Journal* article[28] explored the tragic story of a cluster of teen suicides that took place in Herriman, Utah, over a twelve-month period. Initially, the high school decided not to openly discuss it, fearing it might cause more youth to follow

---

26. Holland, "Like a Broken Vessel," 41.
27. Ibid.
28. Lovett, "One Teenager Killed Himself. Six More Followed."

suit. But the silence neither prevented further suicides nor promoted mental health. In fact, studies show the reverse is true: talking about these tough topics reduces suicide rates and helps those struggling with mental illness find the help they need.

On a daily basis, we should be taking care of our own social, physical, emotional, and spiritual health. No matter your current mental state, creating healthy personal habits in all these areas will build a firm foundation that will be vital throughout your life. Here are some great habits you can work to develop to strengthen your mental health:

1. **Go Outside Every Day.** Feel the sun on your face. Aside from the Vitamin D and psychological boost it will give you, it can decrease anxiety.

2. **Exercise.** In addition to all the good stuff it does for your physical health, exercise is wonderful for mental health too. It can reduce stress, anxiety, ADHD, and improve your sleep. Get out and walk, ride your bike, or hike.

3. **Sleep.** Getting enough sleep is important for your mental health. A functioning circadian rhythm allows the brain to release cortisol in the morning and melatonin to help you fall asleep. On average teens and young adults need eight to ten hours of sleep at night to function optimally in life.[29]

4. **Talk about Your Worries.** When we share our concerns with others, we learn we are not alone. Some of our troubles will evaporate as we talk, and some can only be solved with professional intervention. That's okay. There are people and resources to help us cope with our problems, large and small.[30]

5. **Think of Positive Memories.** Research has found that recalling positive experiences in the past can buffer the negative effects of stress in the present moment.[31]

6. **Practice Self-Compassion.** Give yourself permission to let

---

29. "Sleep in Middle and High School Students." Centers for Disease Control and Prevention.
30. Madsen, "When Worry Becomes a Web of Anxiety and Depression."
31. Hilton, *The Founder of Our Peace*, 43.

go of some of your expectations. You may find you have more time on your hands but are less productive. Or you feel guilty because you know your situation could be worse. Acknowledge your emotions and accept whatever you can do as "good enough," at least for now.

7. **Find a Way to Serve and Connect.** Nothing helps me feel good about myself and my situation like helping others. Check on friends and loved ones, call someone who might be struggling, or visit websites like Just Serve that offer service opportunities.

I also want to make something very clear: If you are struggling with mental health, the people in your life would love to listen and support, including trusted friends, family members, and church leaders. If you need extra help, ask them to connect you with a counselor, therapist, or other professional trained in this area. You can also reach out to a crisis hotline. There are various regional and national resources such as:

- National Suicide Prevention Lifeline: suicidepreventionlifeline. org; 1–800–273–8255 for "24/7, free and confidential support for people in distress, prevention and crisis resources for you or your loved ones, and best practices for professionals."
- Crisis Text Line: crisistextline.org; or text HOME to 741741 (US and Canada), 85258 (UK), or 50808 (Ireland) for free, 24/7 crisis counseling.

If you live in another country or region, a simple internet search should help connect you to resources nearby.

Overall, you can help others by sharing your own struggles to remind friends and family that everyone faces sadness. You can reassure your family and friends that when they fall short of expectations, they are still worthy of our love. You can also advocate in your community for awareness and education on these topics and help those in need find access to the right support. Each of us can help heal and strengthen each other, one hard conversation at a time.

CONCLUSIONS

Although all health and wellness areas—such as emotional, spiritual, social, physical, intellectual, and financial—are important as we work toward preparing ourselves to become leaders, I feel that mental health is front and center in one way or another in most women's lives today. When you (and those around you) realize your own abilities, you can better cope with the normal stresses of life, work productively and effectively, contribute to your community, and enjoy life and be resilient. In short, you can better prepare to become a leader and do the impactful work that our Heavenly Parents know you can do.

Elder Holland concluded his wonderful 2013 general conference talk with this statement: "Trust in God. Hold on in His love. Know that one day the dawn will break brightly and all shadows of mortality will flee. Though we may feel we are 'like a broken vessel,' as the Psalmist says, we must remember, that vessel is in the hands of the divine potter. Broken minds can be healed just the way broken bones and broken hearts are healed. While God is at work making those repairs, the rest of us can help by being merciful, nonjudgmental, and kind."[32] Being merciful, nonjudgmental, and kind are all important characteristics of effective leadership.

---

32. Holland, "Like a Broken Vessel," 41–42.

CHAPTER 14
Mixed Messages

"If God is preparing the women of His Church to fulfill prophecy—both ancient and modern—about the role of women of the Church in these latter days, we should be celebrating and supporting the women in our lives as they prayerfully seek inspiration and use their agency and intelligence to grow spiritually and serve mightily."[1]

—EVA M. WITESMAN,
PROFESSOR, AUTHOR, & SPEAKER

When I speak to women in the Church in different parts of the world, at least a few sisters in each location mention they are surprised that I found so many good quotes from Church leaders on the importance of women influencing and leading. Generally, sisters want to believe that their voices and contributions matter. Most of us want to believe that our lives matter in many settings and that all types of contributions are important to our families, Church congregations, communities, workplaces, and ultimately to our Heavenly Parents. Yet, many women feel that only certain contributions matter in the Church and if you don't fit into a mold of what the

---

1. Witesman, "Women and Education," 7.

"ideal" sister looks like, you aren't valued as highly. Sadly, for some sisters, this is truly their experience.

In reading this book, you may have felt a disconnect between what you are reading and how you see things play out in your own homes, wards, and stakes. For example, chapter 4 talks about the types of leadership opportunities around you, including running for and serving in political elected office; leading efforts to change and improve society; and volunteering for leadership roles in programs or projects led by government, nonprofits, and other types of entities. Yet, you may not see examples of sisters in your wards and stakes who serve in these kinds of roles. You may also occasionally feel that a message you hear from a member of the Church may not feel fair or equitable toward all members. Yet, treating all people with respect and love is continuously preached from the pulpit. These are examples of mixed messages—communication (through words or actions) that sends conflicting information.

Honestly, some people leave the Church because a mixed message may not sit well with them. And yes, sometimes there may be mixed messages around the role of women in the Church. But if our testimonies are grounded in our Savior and in His gospel, we can better see the transformations that are already occurring. Christ needs to be our rock. When our testimonies are firmly planted in the Rock of our Salvation, even if we have questions, we can continue to feel peace. In fact, Sheri L. Dew, in her book *Worth the Wrestle*, stated: "I learned that questions can be instruments of growth. I learned that the Lord will respond to sincere questions. I learned that the humility that accompanies the asking of questions mirrors, though in small measure, the humility demonstrated by the Savior again and again. And I learned that, although there are some answers we don't have, there is no question or issue or problem that the Lord doesn't understand completely, omnipotently. . . . The Lord needs men and women who . . . aren't afraid to wrestle with tough questions."[2] With any mixed message you come across,

---

2. Dew, *Worth the Wrestle*, 5, 31.

I invite you to be prayerful and look to the Savior, who never spoke to or treated women as if they were of less value than men. As you work with your Heavenly Father to see the right path for you—and the divine possibilities for your life—He will continue to prepare you for the future He has in store for you.

THE BOX

Within the Church, mixed messages can be heard and felt through messages from Church leaders, local leaders, or from members in our wards and stakes. Many of these are ingrained in what I call "The Box." Each of us has an invisible box in our minds that contains what we think the "good" or "ideal" Latter-day Saint woman *should* look like or *should* embody. All girls, boys, women, and men have boxes around what young women *should* become, and this is most often unconscious. Here are several examples:

- **Married:** I was raised to believe that the *ideal* woman in the Church is married, and I am not alone in this assumption. I've been told by many single sisters in the Church that they don't feel they belong because they are not married, and they feel "less than" because of this. These sisters may hear "everyone is loved equally by the Lord," but they may not feel that applies to them. Mixed message: You are loved, but you are not quite right because you are not married.
- **No Children:** "Families are forever" is such a strong theme in the Church, and typically the vision we have of families includes children. Couples and single sisters who do not have children often feel less blessed and more judged. In fact, many women who have struggled with infertility have told me they've felt heartbroken by judgmental things that people in Church settings have said. Mixed message: We welcome you at Church, but you need children to fit into the ward family.
- **Faithful Children:** "Good" Latter-day Saint women also have children who are all active and faithful in the Church. The deep heartache this one has caused me personally is hard

to describe. Mixed message: Do everything you can (family home evening, scriptures, church attendance) to teach your children gospel truths, but if they don't stay active you probably did something wrong.

- **Full-Time Homemaker:** Often this ideal Latter-day Saint women "box" can also include being a full-time homemaker, which, through the decades, was preached very openly from the pulpit. In addition, at least in my mind, this "ideal" full-time homemaker always had a clean house, made hot breakfasts for her children each morning, and sent homemade lunches with her kids to school each day. I must admit that if this is truly the measure of success, then I failed miserably. Mixed message: Get personal revelation on what the Lord wants you to do and become, but the "ideal" sister chooses the path of being home full-time.

In addition, that "ideal" sister—at least in my mind through the years—also drives a minivan, loves to bake bread and cook, does crafts and quilts, rejoices when called to work in the nursery and Primary, is soft-spoken and never yells at her kids, and is humble and selfless in every way. I know I'm not alone, as even Patricia T. Holland, former counselor in the Young Women General Presidency, humorously stated that she wasn't the right fit because she wasn't good at sewing: "Can you imagine my burden over the last twenty-five or thirty years 'faking it' in Relief Society sessions?"[3] Sheri L. Dew also admitted to the bishop when he called her to be Relief Society president of a YSA ward in her early twenties, "I don't bake bread, I can't quilt, I love sports."[4]

The trouble with "The Box" is that we often use "ideals" as a measure for the worth of others and we judge them based on these standards. And, even more destructive, we often judge ourselves incredibly harshly based on this "perfect" image as well. I know I rarely practiced self-compassion over the years as I compared myself

---

3. Holland, "One Thing Needful," para. 15.
4. Dew and Pearce, *The Beginning of Better Days*, 34.

to what I thought this "ideal" Latter-day Saint woman was. For many teen and young adult women, these mixed messages—entangled with comparing ourselves and others to whatever we view as "perfection"—are a challenge that can negatively impact our leadership development journey because if we are constantly questioning our worth, then we are reluctant to step forward.

EITHER/OR MENTALITY

Society often gives women two conflicting messages about life choices. This relates to the danger of "either/or" and the power of "and" that I mentioned briefly in previous chapters. Research in Utah has found that many women do not believe they *can* or *should* integrate life roles—that, if they are mothers, they need to be a full-time mother and not finish college, serve in society, or work outside the home in any respect.[5] So, many women choose to drop out of college or university when they marry or have their first child. They also believe they should not plan to become leaders because of this mentality.[6] It breaks my heart that so many amazing women feel they must choose between such good things when the mix of multiple choices could be the best option for them.

As mentioned previously, throughout my life I have received some well-meaning advice implying that I couldn't be a good mother if I was also going to school. However, when my soul felt I needed to prepare for a life of service, I heeded the call. I've endured "either/or" advice related to motherhood and other endeavors—graduate education, part-time jobs, a full-time career, civic engagement, leadership roles, and traveling to speak. I know many other women endure this advice as well, and maybe you have had some of these conversations already too. But let me tell you, personal revelation is the key. It is better to do what God wants you to do than what you believe others

---

5. Madsen and Hanewicz, "The Influence of Religion on a Young Woman's College Decision."
6. Madsen, "Latter-day Saint Women and Leadership: The Influence of Their Religious Worldview, 62.

are expecting you to do. Most of us are familiar with James 1:5, the scripture that led Joseph to receive personal revelation about his life. The same is true for you: "If any of you lack wisdom, let [her] ask of God, that giveth to all [people] liberally, and upbraideth not; and it shall be given [her]." Trust the Lord. He will prepare you to become the leader you are meant to be.

In some ways it may seem easier to just do one thing at a time. I constantly hear women say, "I need to wait until my kids are a certain age" to return to school, run for public office, donate to charities, work on their family histories, and so forth. But life is not all or nothing, and there can be blessings when we thoughtfully add layers to our identities. It's those multiple identities in life that facilitate growth, engage our souls, and give life its savor. I, for one, am grateful for the way my life has been enriched by seeing the power of "and." Although some "box" people may judge you, heeding the call of the "and" can change our lives.[7]

THE HOME

A wonderful 2013 *Ensign* article entitled "Equal Partnership in Marriage" discussed the gospel teachings around equality in marriage. Valerie Hudson, globally known professor and author on gender and national security, and her co-author stated, "Latter-day Saint theology teaches that gender difference does not superimpose a hierarchy between men and women. . . . Social science research supports the prophetic instruction that couples who have an equal partnership have happier relationships, more effective parenting practices, and better-functioning children. Scholars have consistently found that equal partners are more satisfied and have better overall marital quality than couples where one spouse dominates. Equal-partner relationships have less negative interaction and more positive interaction. Moreover, there is evidence that equal partners are more satisfied with the quality of the physical intimacy in their

---

7. Madsen, "Guest Opinion: Women Face the Danger of 'Either/Or' and the Power of 'And.'"

relationship."[8] You also see this language in "The Family: A Proclamation to the World": "In these sacred responsibilities, fathers and mothers are obligated to help one another as equal partners."[9] Yet, some girls and women may experience a mixed message when they don't always see examples of equal partnership in marriages within their own wards and stakes.

THE CHURCH

Sheri L. Dew, former counselor in the General Relief Society Presidency, does a wonderful job of illustrating the confusion young women in the Church often face in the following excerpt: "It can be difficult to know what to prepare for. A young woman may serve a mission IF she desires, but there is no requirement to do so. She is encouraged to get as much education as she can, but she may or may not end up using that education in some kind of professional vocation or career. And some young-adult-age women express concern that if they pursue an education or career they might be sending unintended 'signals' to the Lord that they care more about a profession than about getting married. A woman should develop her talents, but how she will use them may not be clear. She may or may not marry at a traditional age. If she does marry in a 'normal' time frame, she will likely desire to be a mother, but she may or may not be able to bear children. She may or may not choose to work outside the home, but in all likelihood, that decision will be charged with a variety of emotions."[10]

In terms of education, the Church narratives in past decades haven't always helped women feel that advanced education—even at the bachelor's degree level—has been valued. In chapter 8, I discussed the confusing message that young women should prepare for and value motherhood, *and* they should pursue an education, but perhaps not at the expense of motherhood. However, according to the research,

---

8. Hudson and Miller, "Equal Partnership in Marriage," 22.
9. "The Family: A Proclamation to the World," para. 7.
10. Dew, *Women and the Priesthood*, 6–7.

education has countless benefits, including in the home (refer to chapter 8 for the full list of benefits and other details). Fortunately, today we hear current Church leaders emphasizing the importance of college and university degrees for women much more often.

We are also often told that women's voices matter, and even research shows that women's voices are imperative to the best decision making and problem solving (see chapter 3). Yet, we still see situations where women's voices are not included in both Church settings and in society more generally.

At the individual level, some sisters have noted the mixed messages they receive in the Church around Mother in Heaven. On the one hand, the Church does write about the divine role and power of Heavenly Mother and discuss her on the Church website[11] (I mentioned this briefly in chapter 10). But on the other hand, we hear very little about her. In fact, people in Church settings often talk about her quietly, as if we should keep her divine role hidden. Yet, as Valerie Hudson declared, "The whole world, and the whole heaven, changes when we understand She is there."[12]

THE WORKPLACE

Through the years, some sisters have also struggled with mixed messages related to being a full-time homemaker, engaging in paid employment, or doing a mix of both. Of course, this book is about being a leader, including in spaces outside the Church and home. This demonstrates the importance of both listening to current revelation from Church leaders and seeking our own personal revelation. Sometimes I feel called to speak up when I hear these well-meant but hurtful judgments, and women always come up to me after and thank me. Part of being a leader is being willing to speak the truths of women who live outside "The Box."

Because of these messages, many women in the Church experience what Dr. Julie de Azevedo Hanks, a psychotherapist, calls

11. "Mother in Heaven," in *Gospel Topics*.
12. Hudson, "Searching for Heavenly Mother: Why? Why not? How?" para. 23.

"aspirational shame."[13] She explained, "This paradox created . . . the belief that my desire for achievement outside of the home meant that I was not a good woman, not a good mother, not a good wife, and not a good person. I have carried some version of aspirational shame with me for decades." Like Dr. Hanks, I personally struggled with this for years, beating myself up because cooking and sewing did not bring me joy, until I accepted a call from God along with an awareness of a future only He could see for me. He needed me to do work that may not fit into what a "good" or "ideal" sister in the Church would necessarily do.

Overall, I believe it's important to remember Elder Quentin L. Cook's counsel regarding the many decisions women are called to make: "First, no woman should ever feel the need to apologize or feel that her contribution is less significant because she is devoting her primary efforts to raising and nurturing children. Nothing could be more significant in our Father in Heaven's plan. Second, we should all be careful not to be judgmental or assume that sisters are less valiant if the decision is made to work outside the home. We rarely understand or fully appreciate people's circumstances. Husbands and wives should prayerfully counsel together, understanding they are accountable to God for their decisions."[14] We must each decide for ourselves, using personal revelation as a guide, what our pathway should be, and allow others this privilege as well.

CONCLUSION

So, what do we do with these mixed messages? My counsel is that we don't ignore mixed messages, as asking questions and discussing such topics with faithful followers of Christ can help us gain perspectives that can lead to increased faith. As Elder Jeffrey R. Holland of the Quorum of the Twelve Apostles declared: "Honestly acknowledge your questions and your concerns, but first and forever fan the flame of your faith, because all things are possible to them

---

13. Hanks, "Healing Aspirational Shame."
14. Cook, "LDS women are incredible!" 21.

that believe."[15] As our faith grows, we can better prepare to serve and lead.

I truly believe that if we pray and seek revelation, we can reconcile these mixed messages in a way that will allow us to move forward with faith to serve and lead in the kingdom of God. When Christ is our foundation, even if mixed messages arise from time to time, our testimonies can continue to flourish, and we can feel peace. We need to become those "brave, steadfast, and immovable warriors"[16] who influence individuals, families, communities, and societies toward following Him. As Sister Dew declared, "Our influence today can be greater than the influence of any group of women in the history of the world."[17]

---

15. Holland, "Lord, I Believe," 95.
16. Oscarson, "Defenders of the Family Proclamation," 17.
17. Dew, *Women and the Priesthood*, 173.

PART IV

Moving Forward

CHAPTER 15

Personal Revelation

"Be faithful and diligent in keeping the
commandments of God, and I will encircle thee
in the arms of my love . . . Look unto me in every
thought; doubt not, fear not."

—DOCTRINE AND COVENANTS 6:22, 36

Now that we have discussed leadership, preparing to lead, and challenges in the three previous sections of the book, this last part includes two final chapters: "Personal Revelation" and "The Road Less Traveled." Each is important in helping you think carefully about navigating the next steps and moving forward with insight, inspiration, and joy.

Personal revelation has been a rock for me through the years. I have learned about it, yearned for it, asked for it, depended on it, followed it, and found peace because of it. The insights and confirmations I have received from God have been foundational in my decisions—whether minor or substantial—and in my life in general. I'm not perfect by any stretch of the imagination, but I truly depend on promptings that come in a variety of ways. This chapter is personal for me. I believe it is important that I share my own experiences with the hope that they will provide understanding of how you might strengthen your own revelation-receiving efforts and capabilities.

In these last days, it has become critical for us to let our Father reveal His mind and will to each of us as His daughters. As Sheri L. Dew, former counselor in the General Relief Society Presidency, wrote, "If we were born to lead in these latter days (and we were), then we need to understand how God makes His power available to us, what it takes to qualify to receive that power, and how we gain access to that power."[1] Personal revelation is power. Yet, none of us is entitled to it without putting in the work. It takes repentance and forgiveness. It takes effort. It takes persistence. And it takes a believing heart. Personal revelation is particularly important as we prepare for that future only God can see for us.

CHURCH TEACHINGS

In the Church, we have been urged, encouraged, and even commanded to seek personal revelation that can guide our decisions and lives. We hear this at every general conference, and these messages have increased in recent years. For example, President Russell M. Nelson stated, "Pray in the name of Jesus Christ about your concerns, your fears, your weaknesses—yes, the very longings of your heart. And then listen! Write the thoughts that come to your mind. Record your feelings and follow through with actions that you are prompted to take. As you repeat this process day after day, month after month, year after year, you will 'grow into the principle of revelation.'"[2] Asking for and receiving revelation can become a habit if we choose to put in the time and work.

Even if we seek personal revelation, sometimes we may wonder if what we are experiencing is a prompting from the Holy Ghost or just a random warm feeling or thought. I appreciate this direct statement from Elder David A. Bednar of the Quorum of the Twelve Apostles: "How can I tell when I'm being prompted by the Spirit? . . . Quit worrying about it. Quit fussing with it. Quit analyzing it. . . . [If] you honor your covenants [and] . . . keep the commandments . . . I

---

1. Dew, *God Wants a Powerful People*, 22.
2. Nelson, "Revelation for the Church, Revelation For Our Lives," 95.

promise you in the name of the Lord Jesus Christ that as you press forward with faith in Christ, your footsteps will be guided. As you open your mouth, it will be filled, and you will be where you need to be, and most of the time, you will not even have any idea how you got there."[3] I love this! I've always believed that we cannot just stand around "in waiting," as I call it, but we must keep pressing forward "with steadfast faith in Christ" (2 Nephi 31:20). We need to keep moving forward.

I also know people who believe they shouldn't ask for personal revelation unless they feel that they are 100 percent committed, 100 percent believing, and 100 percent secure in their testimony of Christ. However, in the book *Worth the Wrestle*, Sheri L. Dew made some compelling points: "Most spiritual growth, most revelation, most answers to difficult questions requires us to wrestle spiritually.[4] . . . Asking inspired questions leads to knowledge. It leads to revelation. It leads to greater faith. And it leads to peace. Not asking questions, on the other hand, closes off revelation, growth, learning, progression, and the ministering of the Holy Ghost."[5] She also declared, "It is worth wrestling to learn the language of revelation."[6]

And finally, in speaking more broadly about the Holy Ghost, President James E. Faust, former Second Counselor in the First Presidency of the Church, once stated: "I believe the Spirit of the Holy Ghost is the greatest guarantor of inward peace in our unstable world. It can be more mind-expanding and can make us have a better sense of well-being than any chemical or other earthly substance. It will calm nerves; it will breathe peace to our souls. This Comforter can be with us as we seek to improve. It can function as a source of revelation to warn us of impending danger and also keep us from making mistakes. It can enhance our natural sense so that we can see more clearly, hear more keenly, and remember what we

---

3.   Morgenegg, "Living the Gospel Makes You a Better Person," 8.
4.   Dew, *Worth the Wrestle*, 24.
5.   Ibid., 12.
6.   Ibid., 97.

should remember. It is a way of maximizing our happiness."[7] And I would say, don't we all want peace, well-being, safety, clarity, and happiness? I know I do.

BACKGROUND

Personal revelation often comes to people in different ways. I was raised in the Church with a father who worked full-time as a seminary and institute teacher. Both of my parents, Boyd and Helen Willden, were very close to the Spirit and worked with us as children to feel the Spirit. I remember many spiritual experiences that helped guide my early decisions. Serving as a youth leader in my ward and stake throughout my teenage years gave me opportunities to seek revelation. But honestly, picking counselors for presidencies sometimes seemed more logical than spiritual. I remember wondering a few times if I was missing something as names just popped into my mind, and because there weren't many young women in my small city of Moscow, Idaho, it wasn't too hard to pick counselors anyway. However, as is the case for many, I learned a lot about receiving revelation on my full-time mission to Tampa, Florida.

My companions and I were absolutely guided daily on where to go and what to do. I'm so grateful for those eighteen months, so many years ago, as they taught me what it felt like to be guided in the moment, in the hour, in the day, and in the week. I constantly relied on Doctrine and Covenants 9:8–9: "But, behold, I say unto you, that you must study it out in your mind; then you must ask me if it be right, and if it is right I will cause that your bosom shall burn within you; therefore, you shall feel that it is right. But if it be not right you shall have no such feelings, but you shall have a stupor of thought that shall cause you to forget the thing which is wrong; therefore, you cannot write that which is sacred save it be given you from me." I took these verses seriously and followed both the "bosom shall burn" and the "stupor of thought," and I still do today. I use these for both getting witnesses of the Spirit and for guidance

---

7. Faust, "The Gift of the Holy Ghost—A Sure Compass," 5.

on what to do. I believe that each type of impression can be used in different ways. Let me give you an example of both.

BURNING IN THE BOSOM

After my mission I worked at the Missionary Training Center (MTC) in Provo, Utah, and taught new sisters and elders going to English-speaking missions. My brother Mark was also teaching there, so we had many good gospel discussions. He helped me see things in different ways when I was stuck, and I was incredibly "stuck" after the young man I was dating (who became my husband) proposed marriage. I had been home from my mission for a year by then, but I didn't have an interest in marriage. I wanted to get my master's degree first and had other plans as well. In fact, my parents were praying that I would care more about marriage. Although Greg was a good fit for me in many ways, there were a few items on my future husband checklist that were amiss. And yes, I really did have a checklist—probably not the best idea when items were things like "doesn't wear glasses" (he did until he had Lasik surgery ten years ago), "has a father in Church leadership" (his father is not a member), or "sings well" (he loves music, but his singing is . . . well, I'll just leave it at that). I recognize now just how shallow my list was!

In a confused state of mind about this major dilemma, I remember talking to my brother and asking him, "How can you ever know for sure?" Of course, I knew the answer, but he gently reminded me by asking me to grab my scriptures and read Doctrine and Covenants 6:22–23: "Verily, verily, I say unto you, if you desire a further witness, cast your mind upon the night that you cried unto me in your heart, that you might know concerning the truth of these things. Did I not speak peace to your mind concerning the matter? What greater witness can you have than from God?" He then told me that if I did receive the answer that I should marry Greg, I didn't need to worry. I didn't need to ask over and over again because I could just "cast" my mind on that night and remember the answer I had received. I had resisted praying about it, as I didn't want to formally discover God's will, but I finally prayed. As you can guess, I had a spiritual witness that I could not deny. It came in the form of an incredibly strong "burning" in my bosom, which engulfed me from head to toe. The sensation went through my whole body in a way that provided peace (made me cry) and gave me joy (made my heart leap). For me, this type of personal revelation only comes from time to time when the Lord needs to "hit me over the head" to make sure I listened. Others may not need that. But there are other ways the Lord speaks to us, and some people can get hung up waiting for a burning or a still small voice. For some people things just "feel right," and others experience a mental clarity about the right decision. However the Spirit speaks to you, when the decision is right, it will involve a feeling of peace.

STUPOR OF THOUGHT

Earlier in my career I started feeling restless, as I had accomplished most of my goals and I knew I needed a shift. Many people had encouraged me to apply for an associate vice-president position that had opened at my university. It sounded like fun, but I was struggling to get an answer as to whether or not it was the right path. Finally, when the deadline was getting close, I started putting together the extensive application. However, after submitting it, I basically forgot about it. I lost interest and didn't even care about it anymore. I realized that I was having a "stupor of thought," and that was a sign to me that it wasn't the right direction to take. I withdrew my application, and a month later I received personal revelation on a different direction that has led me to the work I'm doing now. This was the path I was supposed to take, and that other position would have gotten me off track. I'm grateful to this day that I paid attention to that "stupor of thought."

I've used the "stupor" a lot through the years. I always have a lot of ideas that could take me in various directions, but many just evaporate away. Sometimes I'll take a step forward in a direction (I'm talking even small things) and if something doesn't feel right I immediately pivot. I don't keep going forward if I feel something is amiss. Sometimes, at least for me, taking some action helps me know whether it is right or whether I should shift. Now, of course, I don't take any steps in directions that are clearly not right. For example, I don't head in any direction contrary to the command we've been given to "stand in Holy places" (D&C 87:8). Overall, I use my mind, my gut (sometimes there is just this feeling that something is amiss), and my heart. I use all of these in the process of studying things out in my mind. And most of the time, my experiences mirror what Elder David A. Bednar taught: "Most frequently, revelation comes in small increments over time and is granted according to our desire, worthiness, and preparation."[8]

INSIGHTS ON INSPIRATION

In some ways, I believe that how your brain and heart work can impact how you might receive personal revelation. I have an active mind, am task-oriented, and have a heart that feels deeply about things I am passionate about. I like keeping busy, and messages from the Spirit occasionally come when I'm in the shower, on a walk, or driving in a car. Often inspiration comes while I'm on my knees, but it just matters what it is, when it needs to come, and what I'm doing at the moment. At times something just feels right, and I know that is the direction to go. Other times ideas come to my mind and I know I need to act because someone needs me—like checking in with one of my children via phone call or text. And now and then I have a question and I listen to a conference talk or read a scripture and then answers come to my mind through the still small voice, or I get a small and quick burning in the bosom. I do need to say, however, that at times the "burning" feels more like a burst of electricity or energy (in a good way). Honestly, it has always been hard for me to describe.

I am always working to increase my spiritual capacity to receive revelation, and I hope you are too. We must all strive to listen more carefully, more often, more deeply, and more profoundly.

---

8. Bednar, "The Spirit of Revelation," 88.

But wherever we currently find ourselves on the continuum of revelation-receiving, I believe this counsel from President Thomas S. Monson is essential to remember: "I have learned that when we heed a silent prompting and act upon it without delay, our Heavenly Father will guide our footsteps and bless our lives and the lives of others. I know of no experience more sweet or feeling more precious than to heed a prompting only to discover that the Lord has answered another's prayer through you."[9]

I believe that inspiration and personal revelation are connected. Becoming the Lord's messenger—even for a moment—could transform your thinking and change your life course toward greater alignment with that "future greater than anything you can imagine" and that "person of glory and light you have potential . . . to become."[10] Personal revelation is entirely up to us. There is no limit! We can pray as much as we want, and we can receive as many personal revelations as we are open to receiving. If we desire to truly know ourselves and more deeply know the mind and will of God, we have that choice. We are the ones who limit ourselves by not seeking and knocking, so "ask, and it shall be given you; seek, and ye shall find; knock, and it shall be opened unto you" (Matthew 7:7).

CONCLUSION

Henry B. Eyring of the First Presidency stated, "Your call began when you were placed into mortality, in a place and time chosen for you by a God who knows you perfectly and loves you as His daughter."[11] I believe that influencing and leading is part of that call. As worthy members of The Church of Jesus Christ of Latter-day Saints, we have so many wonderful gifts that we can harness in our lives to help us prepare. We can use the gift and power of the Holy Ghost, lead and teach by the Spirit, have angels round about us to bear us up, be endowed and sealed in the temple, experience the blessings of

---

9. Monson, "Peace, Be Still," 55.
10. Uchtdorf, "Living the Gospel Joyful," 121.
11. Eyring, "Covenant Women in Partnership with God," 70.

the Atonement, and receive spiritual gifts. And there is a wonderful connection between all of these *and* personal revelation.

With all the gifts, blessings, and opportunities you have been given as sisters in the Church, I agree with Sheri L. Dew when she declared that you have a "sacred obligation to seek after the power of God and then to use that power as He directs,"[12] and that no "spiritual privileges are withheld today from the faithful who seek them repeatedly and diligently."[13] Although God does not typically give us a full picture of what our life is going to look like, He will reveal our next steps, line by line, as we seek, yearn, knock, listen, and receive the revelation that is meant only for us. Personal revelation is the power you need to become who God needs you to become—a leader.

---

12. Dew, *God Wants a Powerful People*, 16–17.
13. Dew, *Worth the Wrestle*, 42.

CHAPTER 16

The Road Less Traveled

Two roads diverged in a yellow wood,
And sorry I could not travel both
And be one traveler, long I stood
And looked down one as far as I could
To where it bent in the undergrowth;
Then took the other, as just as fair,
And having perhaps the better claim,
Because it was grassy and wanted wear;
Though as for that the passing there
Had worn them really about the same,
And both that morning equally lay
In leaves no step had trodden black.
Oh, I kept the first for another day!
Yet knowing how way leads on to way,
I doubted if I should ever come back.
I shall be telling this with a sigh
Somewhere ages and ages hence:
Two roads diverged in a wood, and I—
I took the one less traveled by,
And that has made all the difference.

—ROBERT FROST, "THE ROAD NOT TAKEN"[1]

---

1. Frost, "The Road Not Taken."

The purpose of this book, written specifically for women in The Church of Jesus Christ of Latter-day Saints, is to invite you, encourage you, and support you to take this road less traveled. This is the road that gets you outside your comfort zone and prepares you to gain confidence, find your voice, and become a leader. Always remember that you are a beloved daughter of Heavenly Parents, with "a divine nature and eternal destiny"[2] and that "God sent you here to prepare for a future greater than anything you can imagine."[3]

As I stated in the introduction, you have Heavenly Parents who have a plan for you . . . every single one of you. You have talents, gifts, and strengths that are yours alone. You have a purpose that is crafted for only you, because you are distinct from anyone else. You have the potential to influence those around you for good, and it is vital for each of you to learn to be leaders. Of that I have no doubt. You need to prepare to lead so that you can fulfill your call and help God accomplish His work on earth.

I have felt called to write this book and have loved the journey. Writing it was not an easy process, but I have studied the topics out in my mind and relied on the burning in my bosom and the stupor of thought to guide me (see chapter 15). I've felt led by the Spirit as I have used my head, heart, and hands to do this work—my head because I've been studying these topics for years; my heart because I feel incredibly passionate about the need for this work and my call to assist in moving the work forward; and my hands because I feel compelled to not just think and feel, but to do. I believe in action! I hope reading this book has been a journey for you as well and that you will use your heads, hearts, and hands to make a difference in the way you feel called to.

To help you with this call, part I of this book focused on why God needs you to lead, what leadership is all about, why it is important for women to lead, and the wide variety of ways and places you can influence and lead. Part II focused on how you can prepare to

---

2. "Young Women Theme," para. 1.
3. Uchtdorf, "Living the Gospel Joyful," 121.

influence and lead by strengthening your confidence; discovering your gifts, talents, and strengths; learning about mindsets; pursuing learning and education; exploring your purpose and callings; and understanding your identity. Part III continued by sharing content on a few key challenges you most likely have or will face along your leadership preparation journey: social media, body image, mental health, and mixed messages. And finally, part IV discussed personal revelation and ends with this chapter on the importance of taking the road less traveled. In all, I hope this book has helped you realize that you do not want to "discover too late," as President Henry B. Eyring stated, "that you missed an opportunity to prepare for a future only God could see for you."[4]

GOD NEEDS YOU

As I stated in chapter 1, God needs each of you to prepare now to become a leader. I believe this with all my soul! As you think back to the beginning of the book, I shared three specific quotations that have profoundly influenced my life. First, President Russell M. Nelson stated: "Yet the women of this dispensation are distinct from the women of any other because this dispensation is distinct from any other."[5]

Second, Elder David A. Bednar of the Quorum of the Twelve Apostles, said: "If the Lord is hastening His work, we cannot keep doing things the same way we have always done them."[6]

And finally, well-known Church author Sheri L. Dew wrote: "I believe that the moment we learn to unleash the full influence of converted, covenant-keeping women, the kingdom of God will change overnight."[7] The time is now, and you need to be prepared to influence in ways women in the Church have never influenced before.

God needs us now, so I see urgency in your preparations. President Russell M. Nelson made this powerful statement in 2015:

---

4. Eyring, "Education for Real Life," 18.
5. Nelson, "A Plea to My Sisters," 96.
6. "Apostle instructs hundreds in Uganda," in *Newsroom*.
7. Dew, *Women and the Priesthood*, 164.

"Today . . . we need women who know how to make important things happen by their faith and who are courageous defenders of morality and families in a sin-sick world. We need women who are devoted to shepherding God's children along the covenant path toward exaltation; women who know how to receive personal revelation, who understand the power and peace of the temple endowment; women who know how to call upon the powers of heaven to protect and strengthen children and families; women who teach fearlessly." [8] And I would add that we need women who will use their voices to run and serve in public elected office, speak their minds when things are amiss in society, and stand for what is right in all circumstances, situations, and settings. As "you join with other women of covenant in unity and harmony," President M. Russell Ballard of the Quorum of the Twelve Apostles declared, "there is no limit to your influence for good. . . . Your efforts to nurture in the family, the Church, the school, the community, and in the professional world have been a blessing to many. . . . Once you know the Lord's will, you can then move forward in faith to fulfill your individual purpose." [9]

WE HAVE POWER

President Dallin H. Oaks taught us that "when you are involved in the work of the Lord, the power behind you is always greater than the obstacles before you." [10] As each of us prepares to influence and lead, I believe we have access to assistance that can propel us forward in new and more powerful ways. I will only mention four that are available to all of us if we choose to accept and act:

First, we have power associated with attending the temple and keeping our covenants. In the prayer offered at the dedication of the temple at Kirtland, Ohio, on March 27, 1836, the Prophet Joseph proclaimed: "And we ask thee, Holy Father, that thy servants may

---

8. Nelson, "A Plea to My Sisters," 96–97.
9. Ballard, "Women of Dedication, Faith, Determination, and Action," 2, 4.
10. "Hastening the Work in Europe." *Newsroom*.

go forth from this house armed with thy power, and that thy name may be upon them, and thy glory be round about them, and thine angels have charge over them" (D&C 109:22). Elder M. Russell Ballard also taught: "Every sister who lives as a woman of God becomes a beacon for others to follow and plants seeds of righteous influence that will be harvested for decades to come. Every sister who makes and keeps sacred covenants becomes an instrument in the hands of God."[11]

Second, we have power because of the grace and Atonement of our Savior. Church leaders have taught that because Jesus Christ atoned for our sins, we can feel that impact in our lives and can have more positive impact on others. Sheri L. Dew taught, "His grace is available to us every minute of every hour of every day. . . . Grace is divine enabling power. . . . Tender mercies are always evidence that grace is present. . . . Every divine gift and every spiritual privilege that gives us access to the power of heaven comes from Christ or through Christ or because of Christ, through His grace."[12] And Elder David A Bednar of the Quorum of the Twelve Apostles taught about the enabling power of the Atonement through which we can have "access to strength beyond our natural abilities, our weakness can be turned to strength, and we can know that 'in the strength of the Lord' we can 'do all things' (Alma 20:4)."[13]

Third, our testimonies of Christ can be a source of power in our lives as we seek to develop leadership to better serve Him. In the early history of the restored Church, former General Relief Society President Eliza R. Snow wrote: "I will go forward. . . . I will smile at the rage of the tempest, and ride fearlessly and triumphantly across the boisterous ocean of circumstance. . . . And the 'testimony of Jesus' will light up a lamp that will guide my vision through the portals of immortality, and communicate to my understanding the glories of the Celestial kingdom."[14] I love this!

---

11. Ballard, "Women of Righteousness," 70.
12. Dew, *Amazed By Grace*, 16, 20, 32.
13. Rasmus, "The Enabling Power of the Atonement," 18–21.
14. Snow, *Poems, Religious, Historical, and Political, Vol. 1.*, 148–149.

Finally, we can access the power that comes with help from angels: "And whoso receiveth you, there I will be also, for I will go before your face. I will be on your right hand and on your left, and my Spirit shall be in your hearts, and mine angels round about you, to bear you up" (Doctrine & Covenants 84:88). I appreciate Elder Jeffery R. Holland's declaration that "angels are still sent to help us" and are "dispatched to bless us in time of need,"[15] as well as his guidance that we can ask for angels to help us.[16] However, my favorite is this statement by Joseph Smith in 1842 to the sisters of the Church: "If you live up to your privileges, the angels cannot be restrained from being your associates."[17] I have experienced the miracle of feeling the presence of angels, and it is both humbling and awesome!

MOVING FORWARD

We must be willing to get out of our comfort zones to serve and lead in new, bolder, and braver ways. I love a question that was asked in one of the first Come, Follow Me lessons referring to the scene in the New Testament where Peter steps out of the boat onto the stormy sea: "What is the Lord inviting you to do that might be like stepping out of the boat?"[18] I offer this question to each of you today, tomorrow, and in the days and years to come.

On March 17, 1842, at the first meeting of the Relief Society of Nauvoo, President Emma Smith stated, "We are going to do something extraordinary." I believe that the "we" is the most powerful part of this statement. I am convinced that as each of us prepares to lead, the combined positive influence of committed, covenant-keeping Latter-day Saint women working together will change the world. As President Thomas S. Monson once told the women of the Church, "You are a mighty force for good, one of

---

15. Holland, "The Ministry of Angels," 30.
16. Holland, "Place No More for the Enemy of My Soul," 44.
17. History of the Church, 4:604–5, from a discourse given by Joseph Smith on Apr. 28, 1842, in Nauvoo, Illinois; reported by Eliza R. Snow; see also appendix, page 562, item 3.
18. Come, Follow Me, para 4.

the most powerful in the entire world."[19] And I believe we are just getting started!

As I think about the strength of the women pioneers crossing the plains, I remember the statement that one sister made after the experience was over: "I am thankful that I was counted worthy to be a pioneer."[20] As I think about all the challenges and opportunities we have today, I wonder if similar words come to our minds: "I am grateful I was counted worthy to be a committed, covenant-keeping Latter-day Saint woman in these last days."

In his timeless poem "The Road Not Taken," Robert Frost wrote, "Two roads diverged in a wood, and I—I took the one less traveled by, And that has made all the difference." Preparing to lead, particularly for Latter-day Saint women, is the road less traveled. Oftentimes that road ahead is not clear, and sometimes we need to toss out the plan we created for ourselves. President Russell M. Nelson taught, "We can choose to let God prevail in our lives, or not. We can choose to let God be the most powerful influence in our lives, or not."[21] It is up to us. If we choose God, our preparation to lead can also prepare us to be instruments in His hands.[22] And, when we commit ourselves to Him fully, eagerly, passionately, and courageously, we will find our call, our purpose, true joy, and that future only God can see for us.

---

19. Dew, *Women and the Priesthood*, 23.
20. Lloyd, "Lloyd Family Sketches 1915, 1–2," para. 4
21. Nelson, "Let God Prevail," 92.
22. Nelson, "Let God Prevail."

WORKS CITED

"2015 Plastic Surgery Statistics Report." *American Society of Plastic Surgeons.* 2015. Accessed April 16. 2021. https://d2wirczt3b6wjm.cloudfront.net/ News/Statistics/2015/plastic-surgery-statistics-full-report-2015.pdf.

"Adolescent and Young Adult Health." *World Health Organization.* January 18, 2021. https://www.who.int/news-room/fact-sheets/detail/adolescents-health-risks-and-solutions.

"Adolescent Mental Health." *World Health Organization.* September 28, 2020. https://www.who.int/news-room/fact-sheets/detail/adolescent-mental-health.

"American Society for Aesthetic Plastic Surgery reports more than $13.5 billion spent for the first time ever." American Society for Aesthetic Plastic Surgery. March 8, 2016. *PR Newswire.* http://www.prnewswire.com/news-releases/ american-society-for-aesthetic-plastic-surgery-reports-more-than-135–billion-spent-for-the-first-time-ever-300232768.html.

"Apostle Instructs Hundreds in Uganda." *Newsroom.* January 27, 2014. https:// news-ug.churchofjesuschrist.org/article/apostle-instructs-hundreds-in-uganda.

"Averse Childhood Experiences." *Centers for Disease Control and Prevention.* April 3, 2020. https://www.cdc.gov/violenceprevention/aces/index.html?CDC_AA_refVal=https%3A%2F%2Fwww.cdc.gov%2Fviolenceprevention%-2Facestudy%2Findex.html.

"Complete Health Indicator Report of Depression: Adult Prevalence." *Utah Department of Health.* December 23, 2020. https://ibis.health.utah.gov/ibis-sph-view/indicator/complete_profile/Dep.html.

"Eating Disorder Statistics." *National Association of Anorexia Nervosa and Associated Disorders.* accessed May 8, 2021. https://anad.org/get-informed/ about-eating-disorders/eating-disorders-statistics/.

"Education is a Commandment." *The Church of Jesus Christ of Latter-day Saints*. July 27, 2012. https://www.churchofjesuschrist.org/prophets-and-apostles/ unto-all-the-world/education-is-a-commandment.?lang=eng&_r=1.

"Education." *Gospel Topics*. The Church of Jesus Christ of Latter-day Saints. Accessed May 6, 2021. https://www.churchofjesuschrist.org/study/manual/ gospel-topics/education?lang=eng.

"Goals for the Common Good: Exploring the Impact of Education." *Measure of America* and *United Way*. accessed March 20, 2021. http://www.measureofamerica.org/file/common_good_forecaster_full_report.pdf.

"Hastening the Work in Europe." *Newsroom*. February 18, 2014. https://www. churchofjesuschrist.org/prophets-and-apostles/unto-all-the-world/unto-all-the-world-hastening-the-work-in-europe?lang=eng&clang=bik.

"Latter-day Saints and Education: An Overview." *Newsroom*. Accessed April 20, 2021. https://newsroom.churchofjesuschrist.org/article/mormons-and-education-an-overview.

Lexico Dictionary, s.v., "Imposter Syndrome." Accessed August 2021. https:// www.lexico.com/en/definition/impostor_syndrome

"Mental Health: Strengthening Our Response." *World Health Organization*. March 30, 2018. https://www.who.int/news-room/fact-sheets/detail/mental-health-strengthening-our-response.

"Mental Illness." *National Institute of Mental Health*. Last updated January 2021. https://www.nimh.nih.gov/health/statistics/mental-illness.

"Most Searched Plastic Surgery Procedures by State." *Plastic Surgery Portal*. Accessed May 3, 2021. http://www.plasticsurgeryportal.com/articles/most-searched-plastic-surgery-procedures-by-state.

"Mother in Heaven." *Gospel Topics Essays*. The Church of Jesus Christ of Latter-day Saints. October 2015. https://www.churchofjesuschrist.org/study/ manual/gospel-topics-essays/mother-in-heaven?lang=eng.

"Mother Teresa." *Wikipedia*. Last edited May 10, 2021. https://en.wikipedia.org/ wiki/Mother_Teresa.

"Mothers' Employment Outside the Home." In *Eternal Marriage Student Manual*, 237–240. Salt Lake City: The Church of Jesus Christ of Latter-day Saints. 2003. https://www.churchofjesuschrist.org/study/manual/eternal-marriage-student-manual/mothers-employment-outside-the-home.

"President Nelson about the Church in the Coming Years: 'Eat Your Vitamin Pills. Get Some Rest. It's Going to Be Exciting.'" *LDS Living*. October 31, 2018. https://www.ldsliving.com/President-Nelson-About-the-Church-in-the-Coming-Years-Eat-Your-Vitamin-Pills-Get-Some-Rest-It-s-Going-to-Be-Exciting/s/89632.

"Preventing Suicide." *National Center for Injury Prevention and Control. Division of Violence Prevention*. 2018. https://www.cdc.gov/violenceprevention/pdf/suicide-factsheet.pdf.

"Reaching Every Facet of a Woman's Life: A Conversation with Belle S. Spafford. Relief Society General President." *Ensign*. June 1974. https://www.churchofjesuschrist.org/study/ensign/1974/06/reaching-every-facet-of-a-womans-life?lang=eng.

"Sister Bingham United Nations Transcript: Focus on Faith Briefing Remarks — President Jean B. Bingham." *Newsroom*. 2017. https://newsroom.churchofjesuschrist.org/article/sister-bingham-united-nations-transcript.

"Sleep in Middle and High School Students." *Centers for Disease Control and Prevention*. Last reviewed September 10, 2020. https://www.cdc.gov/healthy-schools/features/students-sleep.htm.

"Social Media and Teens." *American Academy of Child & Adolescent Psychiatry*. Last modified March 2018. https://www.aacap.org/AACAP/Families_and_Youth/Facts_for_Families/FFF-Guide/Social-Media-and-Teens-100.aspx.

"Statistics." *Center of Excellence for Eating Disorders*. University of North Carolina. Accessed April 20, 2021. https://www.med.unc.edu/psych/eatingdisorders/learn-more/about-eating-disorders/statistics/.

"Suicide." *National Institute of Mental Health*. Last updated January 2021. https://www.nimh.nih.gov/health/statistics/suicide.shtml.

"The Family: A Proclamation to the World." *Ensign*. November 1995. 102.

"Viewpoint: Use Social Media Wisely." *Church News*. December 18, 2017. https://www.churchofjesuschrist.org/church/news/viewpoint-use-social-media-wisely?lang=eng.

"Volunteering in the United States. 2015." *U.S. Bureau of Labor Statistics*. February 25, 2016. https://www.bls.gov/news.release/volun.nr0.htm.

"What is Body Image?" *National Eating Disorders Collaboration*. 2017. Accessed May 2, 2021. http://www.nedc.com.au/body-image.

WORKS CITED

"What is Mental Health?" *MentalHealth.gov*. Accessed May 2, 2021. https://www.mentalhealth.gov/basics/what-is-mental-health.

"Women in the Church." *Newsroom*. Accessed March 18, 2021. https://newsroom.churchofjesuschrist.org/article/women-in-the-church.

"Young Women General Presidency: 'What's in a Name?'" *Church News*. November 5, 2020. https://www.thechurchnews.com/leaders-and-ministry/2020–11–05/young-women-general-presidency-class-name-theme-identity-196799.

"Young Women Theme." *The Church of Jesus Christ of Latter-day Saints*. 2019. https://www.churchofjesuschrist.org/study/manual/young-women-theme/young-women-theme?lang=eng.

Aburto, Reyna I. "Thru Cloud and Sunshine, Lord, Abide with Me!" *Liahona*. November 2019. https://media.ldscdn.org/pdf/magazines/liahona-november-2019/2019–11–0000–liahona-eng.pdf?lang=eng.

Aquino, Karl, Steven L. Grover, Barry Goldman, and Robert Folger. "When Push Doesn't Come to Shove: Interpersonal Forgiveness in Workplace Relationships." *Journal of Management Inquiry* 12, no. 3 (2003): 209–216. DOI:10.1177/1056492603256337.

Ashcraft, Catherine, and Anthony Breitzman. "Who Invents It? An Analysis of Women's Participation in Information Technology Patenting." *National Center for Women & Information Technology*. 2007. https://www.ncwit.org/sites/default/files/legacy/pdf/PatentExecSumm.pdf.

Badal, Sangeeta B. "The Business Benefits of Gender Diversity." *Gallup*. January 2014. https://www.gallup.com/workplace/236543/business-benefits-gender-diversity.aspx.

Ballard, M. Russell. "Women of Righteousness." *Ensign*. April 2002. https://media.ldscdn.org/pdf/magazines/ensign-april-2002/2002–04–00–ensign-eng.pdf?lang=eng.

Ballard, M. Russell. "Go for It!" *New Era*. March 2004. https://www.churchofjesuschrist.org/study/new-era/2004/03/go-for-it.

Ballard, M. Russell. "Women of Dedication, Faith, Determination, and Action." *BYU Women's Conference*. May 2015. https://womensconference.byu.edu/sites/womensconference.ce.byu.edu/files/elder_m_russell_ballard_0.pdf.

Ballard, M. Russell. "Precious Gifts from God." *Liahona*. May 2018. https://media.ldscdn.org/pdf/magazines/liahona-may-2018/2018–05–00–liahona-eng.pdf?lang=eng.

Ballard, M. Russell. "Questions and Answers." *BYU Speeches.* Spring 2018. https://magazine.byu.edu/article/questions-and-answers/.

Ballard, M. Russell. *Counseling with Our Councils: Learning to Minister Together in the Church and in the Family (Revised Edition).* Salt Lake City: Deseret Book, 2012.

Bednar, David A. "Marriage Is Essential to His Eternal Plan." *Ensign.* June 2006. https://media.ldscdn.org/pdf/magazines/ensign-june-2006/2006-06-00-ensign-eng.pdf?lang=eng.

Bednar, David A. "The Spirit of Revelation." *General Conference.* April 2011. https://media.ldscdn.org/pdf/general-conference/april-2011-general-conference/2011-04-4050-elder-david-a-bednar-eng.pdf?lang=eng.

Bennis, Warren. G. *On Becoming a Leader.* 4th ed. Philadelphia: Perseus Books Group, 2009.

Benson, Joanna, and Lara Jackson. "Nobody's Perfect: A Look at Toxic Perfectionism and Depression." *The Millennial Star.* March 21, 2013. https://www.millennialstar.org/nobodys-perfect-a-look-at-toxic-perfectionism-and-depression.

Bert, Fabrizio, Maria R. Gualano, Elisa Camussi, and Roberta Siliquini. "Risks and Threats of Social Media Websites: Twitter and the Proana Movement. *Cyberpsychology, Behavior and Social Networking* 19. no. 4 (2016): 233–238. https://iris.unito.it/handle/2318/1588562#.X4iAKdBKiUl.

Bingham, Jean B. "How Vast is Our Purpose." *BYU Women's Conference.* May 5, 2017. https://www.churchofjesuschrist.org/callings/relief-society/messages-from-leaders/bingham-womens-conference-2017?lang=eng.

Bingham, Jean B. "Women and Covenant Power." *Liahona.* January 2021. https://media.ldscdn.org/pdf/magazines/liahona-january-2021/17463-2021-01-0014-women-and-covenant-power-eng.pdf?lang=eng.

Bingham, Jean B. "Women of Covenant: The Importance of Seeking and Acting on Revelation." *Church News.* May 13, 2020. https://www.churchofjesuschrist.org/church/news/women-of-covenant-the-importance-of-seeking-and-acting-on-revelation?lang=eng.

Boardman, Jason D., Daniel A. Powers, Yolanda C. Padilla, and Robert A. Hummer. "Low Birth Weight, Social Factors, and Developmental Outcomes among Children in the United States." *Demography* 39, no. 2 (2002): 358–368.

Borysenko, Joan. "Proverbial Wisdom." *Quoteland.com*. Accessed April 2021. http://www.quoteland.com/author/Joan-Borysenko-Quotes/228/.

Brennfleck, Kevin and Brennfleck, Kay M. *Live Your Calling: A Practical Guide to Finding and Fulfilling Your Mission in Life*. San Francisco: Jossey-Bass, 2005.

Buckingham, Marcus and Donald O. Clifton. *Now, Discover Your Strengths*. Washington, D.C.: Free Press, 2001.

Buechner, Frederick. *Wishful Thinking: A Seeker's ABC*. New York: Harper & Row, 1973.

Cambridge Dictionary Online, s.v., "identity." Accessed April 15, 2021. https://dictionary.cambridge.org/dictionary/english/identity.

Carlson, Richard. "Richard Carlson Quote." In Lib Quotes. https://libquotes.com/richard-carlson/quote/lbp4x8a.

Catalyst. "Infographic: The Double-Bind Dilemma for Women in Leadership." August 2, 2018. https://www.catalyst.org/research/infographic-the-double-bind-dilemma-for-women-in-leadership/.

Catalyst. "Tool: Why Diversity Matters." July 23, 2013. http://www.catalyst.org/knowledge/why-diversity-matters.

Chittister, Joan. "We Are at a Crossroads for Women in the Church." *National Catholic Reporter*. December 11, 2013. https://www.ncronline.org/blogs/where-i-stand/we-are-crossroads-women-church.

Churchill, Winston. "A Man's Finest Hour." August 30, 2011. https://theimaginativeconservative.org/2011/08/quote-of-day-mans-finest-hour.html.

Clerkin, Cathleen and Meena S. Wilson. "Gender Differences in Developmental Experiences." In *Handbook of Research on Gender and Leadership*. 378–394. Cheltenham: Edward Elgar, 2017.

Collier, Stephanie. "Should We Screen All Adolescent Girls and Women for Anxiety?" *Harvard Health Blog*. August 14, 2020. https://www.health.harvard.edu/blog/should-we-screen-all-adolescent-girls-and-women-for-anxiety-2020081420754.

Come, Follow Me. Salt Lake City: Intellectual Reserve, 2019. https://www.churchofjesuschrist.org/study/manual/come-follow-me-for-individuals-and-families-new-testament-2019/13?lang=eng.

Cook, Mary N. "Seek Learning: You Have a Work to Do." *Liahona*. May 2012. https://media.ldscdn.org/pdf/lds-magazines/liahona-may-2012/2012–05–00–liahona-eng.pdf?lang=eng.

Cook, Quentin L. "LDS Women are Incredible!" *Ensign*. May 2011. https://media.ldscdn.org/pdf/magazines/ensign-may-2011/2011–05–00–ensign-eng.pdf?lang=eng.

Craddock, Nadia, Phillippa Diedrichs, Amy Slater, Caterina Gentili, Maia Thornton, Helena L. Smith, and Kristy Garbett. "Written Evidence Submitted by the Centre for Appearance Research (MISS0045)." *The Centre for Appearance Research*. July 23. 2020. https://committees.parliament.uk/writtenevidence/7943/pdf/.

Dalton, Elaine S. "Now is the Time to Arise and Shine!" *Liahona*. May 2012. https://www.churchofjesuschrist.org/study/general-conference/2012/04/now-is-the-time-to-arise-and-shine?lang=eng.

Dalton, Elaine S. *No Ordinary Women: Making a Difference through Righteous Influence*. Salt Lake City: Deseret Book, 2016.

Daughters in My Kingdom: The History and Work of Relief Society. Salt Lake City: The Church of Jesus Christ of Latter-day Saints. 2011. https://www.churchofjesuschrist.org/study/manual/daughters-in-my-kingdom-the-history-and-work-of-relief-society.

DeHoyos, Genevieve. *Stewardship—The Divine Order*. Bountiful: Horizon, 1982.

DeRue, D. Scott, and Susan J. Ashford. "Who Will Lead and Who Will Follow? A Social Process of Leadership Identity Construction in Organizations." *The Academy of Management Review* 35, no. 4 (2010): 627–647.

Desilver, Drew. "The Concerns and Challenges of Being a U.S. Teen: What the Data Show." *Pew Research Center FactTank*. February 26, 2019. https://www.pewresearch.org/fact-tank/2019/02/26/the-concerns-and-challenges-of-being-a-u-s-teen-what-the-data-show/.

DeTavis, Hannah. "Rethinking Beauty: A Gospel Perspective on Body Image." *Ensign*. August 2019. August). https://www.churchofjesuschrist.org/study/ensign/2019/08/young-adults/rethinking-beauty-a-gospel-perspective-on-body-image?lang=eng.

Dew, Sheri L. and Virginia H. Pearce. *The Beginning of Better Days: Divine Instruction to Women from the Prophet Joseph Smith*. Salt Lake City: Deseret Book, 2012.

Dew, Sheri L. "It Is Not Good for Man or Woman to Be Alone." *General Conference*. October 2001. https://www.churchofjesuschrist.org/study/general-conference/2001/10/it-is-not-good-for-man-or-woman-to-be-alone?lang=eng.

Dew, Sheri L. *Amazed by Grace*. Salt Lake City: Deseret Book, 2015.

Dew, Sheri L. *God Wants a Powerful People*. Salt Lake City: Deseret Book, 2007.

Dew, Sheri L. *Women and the Priesthood: What One Woman Believes*. Salt Lake City: Deseret Book, 2013.

Dew, Sheri L. *Worth the Wrestle*. Salt Lake City: Deseret Book, 2017.

Dictionary.com Online, s.v., "identity." Accessed April 15, 2021. https://www.dictionary.com/browse/identity.

Dilworth, Robert L. "Creating Opportunities for Reflection in Action Learning: Nine Important Avenues." *ITAP International*. Accessed March 10, 2021. http://www.itapintl.com.cn/indexphp/about-us/articles/creating-opportunities-for-reflection-in-action-learning.htm.

Dweck, Carol S. "Can Personality Be Changed? The Role of Beliefs in Personality and Change." *Current Directions in Psychological Science* 17, no. 6 (2008): 391–394.

Dweck, Carol S. *Mindset: The New Psychology of Success*. New York City: Ballantine Books, 2016.

Emelianova, Olga and Christina Milhomem. "Women on Boards: 2019 Progress Report." *MSCI*. December 2019. https://www.msci.com/documents/10199/29f5bf79–cf87–71a5–ac26–b435d3b6fc08.

Eubank, Sharon. "By Union of Feeling We Obtain Power with God." *General Conference*. October 2020. https://media.ldscdn.org/pdf/2020–10–3010–sharon-eubank-eng.pdf?lang=eng.

Eubank, Sharon. "The Status of Women Worldwide" (Speech, Utah Women's Leadership Speaker & Dialogue Series. Utah Valley University. Orem. February 19, 2020). https://www.youtube.com/watch?v=SqWfRaDsB04.

Eubank, Sharon. "Turn on Your Light." *Liahona*. November 2017. https://media.ldscdn.org/pdf/magazines/liahona-november-2017/2017–11–00–liahona-eng.pdf?lang=eng.

Eyring, Henry B. "Covenant Women in Partnership with God." *Liahona*. November 2019. https://www.churchofjesuschrist.org/study/general-conference/2019/10/34eyring?lang=eng.

Eyring, Henry B. "Education for Real Life." *Ensign*. October 2002. https://media.ldscdn.org/pdf/magazines/ensign-october-2002/2002–10–00–ensign-eng.pdf?lang=eng.

Eyring, Henry B. "Sisters in Zion." *General Conference*. October 2020. https://www.churchofjesuschrist.org/study/general-conference/2020/10/35eyring?lang=eng.

Eyring, Henry B. "Women and Gospel Learning in the Home." *Liahona*. November 2018. https://media.ldscdn.org/pdf/magazines/liahona-november-2018/2018–11–0000–liahona-eng.pdf?lang=eng.

Farh, Crystal I. C., Jo K. Oh, John R. Hollenbeck, Andrew Yu, Stephanie M. Lee, and Danielle D. King. "Token Female Voice Enactment in Traditionally Male-Dominated Teams: Facilitating Conditions and Consequences for Performance." *Academy of Management Journal* 63, no. 3 (2020). https://doi.org/10.5465/amj.2017.0778.

Faust, James E. "The Gift of the Holy Ghost—A Sure Compass." *General Conference*. April 1989. https://www.churchofjesuschrist.org/study/general-conference/1989/04/the-gift-of-the-holy-ghost-a-sure-compass?lang=eng.

First Presidency of the Church. "The Origin of Man." *Improvement Era*. November 1909. https://media.ldscdn.org/pdf/magazines/ensign-february-2002/2002–02–00–ensign-eng.pdf?lang=eng.

Frost, Robert. "The Road Not Taken." Poetry Foundation. Accessed May 4. 2021. https://www.poetryfoundation.org/poems/44272/the-road-not-takenFellingham.

Gallivan, Heather R. "Teens, Social Media and Body Image." *Park Nicollet Melrose Center*. 2014. https://www.macmh.org/wp-content/uploads/2014/05/18_Gallivan_Teens-social-media-body-image-presentation-H-Gallivan-Spring-2014.pdf.

Gallup. "What is the Difference Between a Talent and a Strength?" *CliftonStrengths for Students*. https://www.strengthsquest.com/help/general/143096/difference-talent-strength.aspx.

Gardner, Barbara M. "Connecting Daughters of God with His Priesthood Power." *Ensign*. March 2019. https://media.ldscdn.org/pdf/magazines/ensign-march-2019/2019–03–0010–connecting-daughters-of-god-with-his-priesthood-power-eng.pdf?lang=eng.

Gates, Susa Y. "The Vision Beautiful." *Improvement Era* 23, no. 6 (1920): 542–543. https://archive.bookofmormoncentral.org/content/vision-beautiful.

Gerzema, John and Michael D'Antonio. *The Athena Doctrine: How Women (and the Men Who Think Like Them) Will Rule the Future*. San Francisco: Jossey-Bass, 2013.

Gramlich, John. "What the 2020 Electorate Looks Like by Party, Race and Ethnicity, Age, Education, and Religion." *Pew Research Center*. October 26, 2020. https://www.pewresearch.org/fact-tank/2020/10/26/what-the-2020-electorate-looks-like-by-party-race-and-ethnicity-age-education-and-religion/.

Grellet, Etienne de. "Etienne de Grellet Quotes." *GoodReads*. Accessed May 5, 2021. https://www.goodreads.com/author/quotes/6886793.Etienne_de_Grellet.

Hafen, Marie K. "Celebrating Womanhood." *Ensign*. June 1992. https://www.churchofjesuschrist.org/study/ensign/1992/06/celebrating-womanhood?lang=eng.

Hagan, Lisa K., and Janet Kuebli. "Mothers' and Fathers' Socialization of Preschoolers' Physical Risk Taking." *Journal of Applied Developmental Psychology* 28, no. 1 (2007): 2–14. https://doi.org/10.1016/j.appdev.2006.10.007.

Handford, Charlotte M., Ronald M. Rapee, and Jasmine Fardouly. "The Influence of Maternal Modeling on Body Image Concerns and Eating Disturbances in Preadolescent Girls." *Behavior Research and Therapy* 100 (January 2018): 17–23. https://www.sciencedirect.com/science/article/abs/pii/S0005796717302309.

Hanks, Julie D. "Healing Aspirational Shame." *Aspiring Mormon Women*. 2015. http://aspiringmormonwomen.org/2015/07/02/healing-aspirational-shame/.

Higgs, Malcolm, Ulrich Plewnia, and Jorg Ploch. "Influence of Team Composition and Task Complexity on Team Performance." *Team Performance Management* 11, no. 7/8 (2005): 227–250.

Hilton III, John. *The Founder of Our Peace: Christ-Centered Patterns for Easing Worry, Stress, and Fear*. Salt Lake City: Deseret Book. 2020.

Hinckley, Gordon B. "How Can I Become the Woman of Whom I Dream? *Ensign*. May 2001. https://www.churchofjesuschrist.org/study/ensign/2001/05/how-can-i-become-the-woman-of-whom-i-dream?lang=eng.

Hinckley, Gordon B. "Stand Up for Truth." *BYU Speeches*. September 17, 1996. https://speeches.byu.edu/wp-content/uploads/pdf/Hinckley_Gordon_1996_09.pdf.

Hinckley, Gordon B. "Inspirational Thoughts." *Ensign*. June 1999. https://www.churchofjesuschrist.org/study/ensign/1999/06/inspirational-thoughts?lang=eng.

Hinckley, Gordon B. "Ten Gifts from the Lord" (October 1985 general conference). https://www.churchofjesuschrist.org/study/general-conference/1985/10/ten-gifts-from-the-lord?lang=eng.

History of the Church. 4:604–5; from a discourse given by Joseph Smith on Apr. 28, 1842, in Nauvoo, Illinois; reported by Eliza R. Snow; see also appendix, page 562, item 3.

Holland, Jeffrey R. "Like a Broken Vessel." *Ensign.* October 2013. https://ia800401.us.archive.org/29/items/Ensign_Magazine-2013–11/Ensign_Magazine-2013–11.pdf.

Holland, Jeffrey R. "Lord, I Believe." *Liahona.* May 2013. https://media.ldscdn.org/pdf/magazines/liahona-may-2013/2013–05–00–liahona-eng.pdf?lang=eng.

Holland, Jeffrey R. "The Ministry of Angels." *Ensign.* November 2008. https://ia600405.us.archive.org/28/items/Ensign_Magazine-2008–11/Ensign_Magazine-2008–11.pdf.

Holland, Jeffrey R. "To Young Women." *Ensign.* November 2005. https://ia800409.us.archive.org/2/items/Ensign_Magazine-2005–11/Ensign_Magazine-2005–11.pdf.

Holland, Jeffrey R. *To My Friends: Message of Counsel and Comfort.* Salt Lake City: Deseret Book, 2015.

Holland, Jeffrey R. "Place No More for the Enemy of My Soul" (April 2010 general conference). https://media.ldscdn.org/pdf/general-conference/april-2010–general-conference/2010–04–2090–elder-jeffrey-r-holland-eng.pdf?lang=eng.

Holland, Patricia T. "One Thing Needful: Becoming Women of Greater Faith in Christ." *Ensign.* October 1987. https://www.churchofjesuschrist.org/study/ensign/1987/10/one-thing-needful-becoming-women-of-greater-faith-in-christ?lang=eng.

Holmes, Oliver W. "Quotable Quote." *GoodReads.* https://www.goodreads.com/quotes/135802–every-calling-is-great-when-greatly-pursued.

House of Commons Women and Equalities Committee. "Body Image Survey Results: First Special Report of Session 2019–21." September 22, 2020. https://committees.parliament.uk/publications/2691/documents/26657/default/.

House of Commons Women and Equalities Committee. "Changing the Perfect Picture: An Inquiry into Body Image: Sixth Report of Session 2019–21."

March 21, 2021. https://committees.parliament.uk/publications/5357/documents/53751/default/.

Hudson, Valerie M., and Richard B. Miller. "Equal Partnership in Marriage." *Ensign.* April 2013. https://media.ldscdn.org/pdf/magazines/ensign-april-2013/2013–04–09–equal-partnership-in-marriage-eng.pdf?lang=eng.

Hudson, Valerie M. "Searching for Heavenly Mother: Why? Why not? How?" *Faith Matters.* November 10, 2019. https://faithmatters.org/searching-for-heavenly-mother-why-why-not-how/.

Hunter, Howard W. "To the Women of the Church." *General Conference.* October 1992. https://www.churchofjesuschrist.org/study/general-conference/1992/10/to-the-women-of-the-church?lang=eng.

Hurley, Casey. "What If "Plan A" Doesn't Work? Helping Female Students Navigate an Uncertain Life Course." *Perspective.* Autumn 2007. https://www.byui.edu/a/69368.

Ibarra, Herminia, and Otilia Obodaru. "Women and the Vision Thing." *Harvard Business Review.* January 2009. https://hbr.org/2009/01/women-and-the-vision-thing/ar/1.

Karpowitz, Christopher F., and Tali Mendelberg. *The Silent Sex: Gender. Deliberation. and Institutions.* Princeton: Princeton University Press, 2014.

Kay, Katty, and Claire Shipman. "The Confidence Gap." *The Atlantic.* May 2014. https://www.theatlantic.com/magazine/archive/2014/05/the-confidence-gap/359815/.

Kay, Katty, and Claire Shipman. *The Confidence Code: The Science and Art of Self-Assurance—What Women Should Know.* New York City: Harper Business, 2014.

Kelly, Yvonne, Afshin Zilanawala, Cara Booker, and Amanda Sacker. "Social Media Use and Adolescent Mental Health: Findings from the UK Millennium Cohort Study. *EClinicalMedicine* 6 (2008): 59–68. https://doi.org/10.1016/j.eclinm.2018.12.005.

Kennedy, Robert F. "Day of Affirmation Address. University of Capetown, Capetown, South Africa." John F. Kennedy Presidential Library and Museum. June 6, 1966. https://www.jfklibrary.org/learn/about-jfk/the-kennedy-family/robert-f-kennedy/robert-f-kennedy-speeches/day-of-affirmation-address-university-of-capetown-capetown-south-africa-june-6–1966.

Kimball, Spencer W. "Jesus: The Perfect Leader." *Ensign*. August 1979. https://www.churchofjesuschrist.org/study/ensign/1979/08/jesus-the-perfect-leader?lang=eng.

Kimball, Spencer W. "The Role of Righteous Women." *General Conference*. October 1979. https://www.churchofjesuschrist.org/study/general-conference/1979/10/the-role-of-righteous-women?lang=eng.

Kite, Lexie, and Lindsay Kite. "More Than a Body: Seeing as God Sees." *New Era*. August 2019. https://media.ldscdn.org/pdf/magazines/new-era-august-2019/2019–08–0003–more-than-a-body-seeing-as-god-sees-eng.pdf?lang=eng.

Kite, Lexie, and Lindsay Kite. *More Than a Body: Your Body is an Instrument. Not an Ornament*. Boston: Houghton Mifflin Harcourt, 2021.

Lloyd, Susannah S. "Lloyd Family Sketches 1915, 1-2." Pioneer Database 1847–1868. https://history.churchofjesuschrist.org/overlandtravel/sources/7446/lloyd-susannah-stone-lloyd-family-sketches-1915-1-2.

Lopez, Shane J., Jennifer T. Pedrotti, and Snyder, C. R. *Positive Psychology: The Scientific and Practical Explorations of Human Strengths*. 2nd ed. Thousand Oakes: SAGE Publishing. 2011.

Lovett, Ian. "One Teenager Killed Himself. Six More Followed." *The Wall Street Journal*. April 12, 2019. https://www.wsj.com/articles/one-teenager-killed-himself-six-more-followed-11555061402.

Luxton, David D., Jennifer D. June, and Jonathan M. Fairall. "Social Media and Suicide: A Public Health Perspective." *American Journal of Public Health* 102, no. S2 (2012): S195–S200.

Ma, Jennifer, Matea Pender, and Meredith Welch. "Education Pays 2019: The Benefits of Higher Education for Individuals and Society." *CollegeBoard*. 2019. https://research.collegeboard.org/pdf/education-pays-2019–full-report.pdf.

Madsen, Susan R., and Cheryl Hanewicz. "The Influence of Religion on a Young Woman's College Decision." *Utah Women & Leadership Project. Research Snapshot*. April 2011. https://www.usu.edu/uwlp/files/snapshot/10.pdf.

Madsen, Susan R. "Guest Op-ed: The Gift of Forgiveness." *Standard-Examiner*. December 21, 2020. https://www.standard.net/opinion/guest-commentary/guest-op-ed-the-gift-of-forgiveness/article_bd2ba4b3–f428–5a08–97e6–118855a684c5.html.

Madsen, Susan R. "Guest Opinion: Women Face the Danger of 'Either/Or' and the Power of 'And.'" *The Salt Lake Tribune*. November 26, 2019. https://www.sltrib.com/opinion/commentary/2019/11/26/susan-r-madsen-women-face/.

Madsen, Susan R. "Honor International Women's Day by Becoming Empowered as Global Citizens." *The Daily Herald*. March 24, 2020. https://www.heraldextra.com/news/opinion/local-guest-opinions/madsen-honor-international-women-s-day-by-becoming-empowered-as/article_7f036edc-d21b-5d93–8342–f02790b8ee26.html.

Madsen, Susan R. "Latter-day Saint Women and Leadership: The Influence of Their Religious Worldview. *Journal of Leadership Education* 15, no. 2 (2016): 58–73. https://journalofleadershiped.org/jole_articles/latter-day-saint-women-and-leadership-the-influence-of-their-religious-worldview/.

Madsen, Susan R. "Leadership Responsibility and Calling: The Role of Calling in a Woman's Choice to Lead." In *Responsible Leadership: Realism and Romanticism*. 89–107. Oxon: Routledge, 2016.

Madsen, Susan R. "Strengthen Your Growth Mindset: Using this Uncertain Time for Learning." *LinkedIn*. April 24, 2020. https://www.linkedin.com/pulse/strengthen-your-growth-mindset-using-uncertain-time-learning-madsen/?published=t.

Madsen, Susan R. "The Key to Leadership Development is Critical Reflection." *Forbes*. May 26, 2020. https://www.forbes.com/sites/forbescoachescouncil/2020/05/26/the-key-to-leadership-development-is-critical-reflection.

Madsen, Susan R. "When Worry Becomes a Web of Anxiety and Depression." *The Salt Lake Tribune*. May 27, 2020. https://www.sltrib.com/opinion/commentary/2020/05/27/susan-r-madsen-when-worry/.

Madsen, Susan R. "Why Do We Need More Women Leaders in Utah?" Research & Policy Brief no. 10. January 12, 2015. Utah Women & Leadership Project. https://www.usu.edu/uwlp/files/briefs/10–why-do-we-need-more-women-leaders.pdf.

Madsen, Susan R., Janika Dillon, and Robbyn T. Scribner. "Cosmetic Surgery and Body Image among Utah Women." *Utah Women & Leadership Project. Research Snapshot*. April 10, 2017. https://www.usu.edu/uwlp/files/snapshot/20.pdf.

Madsen, Susan R., Cheryl Hanewicz, Susan Thackeray, and David King. "A Glimpse at Women and Higher Education in Utah. *SquareTwo* 3, no. 3 (2010). http://squaretwo.org/Sq2ArticleMadsenEducation.html.

Madsen, Susan R., Robbyn Scribner, Wendy Fox-Kirk, and Sara M. Lafkas. "The Leadership Development Gained by Women Serving Full-time Missions." *Research & Policy Brief No. 21. Utah Women & Leadership Project.* January 7, 2020. https://www.usu.edu/uwlp/files/briefs/21-leadership-development-full-time-missions.pdf.

Mayo Clinic. "Anorexia Nervosa." February 20, 2018. https://www.mayoclinic.org/diseases-conditions/anorexia-nervosa/symptoms-causes/syc-20353591.

Mayo Clinic. "Depression (Major Depressive Disorder)." February 3, 2018. https://www.mayoclinic.org/diseases-conditions/depression/symptoms-causes/syc-20356007.

Mayo Clinic. "Teens and Social Media Use: What's the Impact?" December 21, 2019. https://www.mayoclinic.org/healthy-lifestyle/tween-and-teen-health/in-depth/teens-and-social-media-use/art-20474437.

McBaine, Neylan. *Women at Church: Magnifying LDS Women's Local Impact.* Salt Lake City: Greg Kofford Books, 2014.

McCambridge, Jim, John McAlaney, and Richard Rowe. "Adult Consequences of Late Adolescent Alcohol Consumption: A Systematic Review of Cohort Studies." *PLoS Medicine* 8, no. 2 (2011). https://doi.org/10.1371/journal.pmed.1000413

Mehrabian, Albert. *Silent Messages: Implicit Communication of Emotions and Attitudes.* Beverly: Wadsworth, 1981.

Merriam-Webster Online, s.v., "identity." Accessed April 15, 2021. https://www.merriam-webster.com/dictionary/identity.

Merriam-Webster Online, s.v., "purpose." Accessed April 15. 2020. https://www.merriam-webster.com/dictionary/purpose.

Monson, Thomas S. "Life's Greatest Decisions." *BYU Speeches.* September 7, 2003. https://media.ldscdn.org/pdf/ces-firesides/2003-ces-firesides-for-young-adults/2003-09-04-lifes-greatest-decisions-eng.pdf?download=true.

Monson, Thomas S. "Peace, Be Still." *Ensign.* October 2002. https://ia800403.us.archive.org/1/items/Ensign_Magazine-2002-11/Ensign_Magazine-2002-11.pdf.

Monson, Thomas S. "Three Goals to Guide You." *Ensign.* November 2007. https://media.ldscdn.org/pdf/magazines/ensign-november-2007/2007-11-00-ensign-eng.pdf?lang=eng.

Morgenegg, Ryan. "Living the Gospel Makes You a Better Person." *Church News*. May 2014. https://www.thechurchnews.com/archives/2014–05–17/living-the-gospel-makes-you-a-better-person-40179.

Murphy, Heather. "Picture a Leader. Is She a Woman?" *The New York Times*. March 16, 2018. https://www.nytimes.com/2018/03/16/health/women-leadership-workplace.html.

Namie, Joylin. "'In the World. But Not of the World': The Paradox of Plastic Surgery among Latter-day Saint Women in Utah." *The Journal of the Utah Academy of Sciences, Arts, & Letters* 90 (2013): 225–248.

Nelson, Russell M. "A Plea to My Sisters." *Ensign*. November 2015. https://media.ldscdn.org/pdf/general-conference/october-2015–general-conference/2015–00–complete-conference-eng.pdf?lang=eng.

Nelson, Russell M. "Education: A Righteous Responsibility." *BYU Idaho Devotionals*. 2010. https://www.byui.edu/devotionals/elder-russell-m-nelson-winter-2010.

Nelson, Russell M. "Let God Prevail" (October 2020 general conference). https://media.ldscdn.org/pdf/2020–10–4060–russell-m-nelson-eng.pdf?lang=eng.

Nelson, Russell M. "Reflection and Resolution." *BYU Speeches*. January 7, 2004. https://speeches.byu.edu/talks/russell-m-nelson/reflection-resolution/.

Nelson, Russell M. "Revelation for the Church. Revelation for Our Lives." *Ensign*. May 2018. https://media.ldscdn.org/pdf/magazines/ensign-may-2018/2018–05–00–ensign-eng.pdf?lang=eng.

Nelson, Russell M. "Sisters' Participation in the Gathering of Israel." *Ensign*. October 2018. https://media.ldscdn.org/pdf/magazines/ensign-november-2018/2018–11–0000–ensign-eng.pdf?lang=eng.

Nelson, Russell M. "Spiritual Treasures." *Ensign*. November 2019. https://media.ldscdn.org/pdf/magazines/ensign-november-2019/2019–11–0000–ensign-eng.pdf?lang=eng.

Northouse, Peter G. *Leadership: Theory and Practice*. 8th ed. Thousand Oakes: SAGE Publications, 2018.

Oaks, Dallin H. "Women and Education." *Ensign*. March 1975. https://www.churchofjesuschrist.org/study/ensign/1975/03/insights/women-and-education?lang=eng.

Oates, Kerris L. M., M. Elizabeth Lewis Hall, Tamara L. Anderson, and Michele M. Willingham. "Pursuing Multiple Callings: The Implications of Balancing Career and Motherhood for Women and the Church." *Journal of Psychology and Christianity* 27, no. 3 (2008): 227–257.

Office of Disease Prevention and Health Promotion. "Mental Health." Accessed May 13, 2021. https://www.healthypeople.gov/2020/leading-health-indicators/2020–lhi-topics/Mental-Health.

Oscarson, Bonnie L. "Defenders of the Family Proclamation." *Liahona.* May 2015. https://media.ldscdn.org/pdf/magazines/liahona-may-2015/2015–05–00–liahona-eng.pdf?lang=eng.

Oscarson, Bonnie L. "Rise Up in Strength, Sisters in Zion." *Ensign.* November 2016. https://media.ldscdn.org/pdf/magazines/ensign-november-2016/2016–11–00–ensign-eng.pdf?lang=eng

Oscarson, Bonnie L. "The Needs Before Us." *Ensign.* October 2017. https://media.ldscdn.org/pdf/magazines/ensign-november-2017/2017–11–00–ensign-eng.pdf?lang=eng.

Oscarson, Bonnie L. "Young Women in the Work." *Ensign.* May 2018. https://media.ldscdn.org/pdf/magazines/ensign-may-2018/2018–05–00–ensign-eng.pdf?lang=eng.

Pak, Richard, and Steve Kroes. "Lifetime Value of a College Degree." Utah Foundation. February 2006. http://www.utahfoundation.org/uploads/2006_01_value_degree.pdf.

Palmer, Parker J. *Let Your Life Speak: Listening for the Voice of Vocation.* San Francisco: Jossey-Bass, 2000.

Pascarella, Ernest T., and Patrick T. Terenzini. *How College Affects Students: A Third Decade of Research.* San Francisco: Jossey-Bass, 2005.

Peale, Norman V. "Believe in Yourself." PassItOn. Accessed May 13, 2021. https://www.passiton.com/inspirational-quotes/4522–one-of-the-greatest-moments-in-anybodys.

Pew Research Center. "How Americans View Their Jobs." October 6, 2016. 54–62. https://www.pewresearch.org/social-trends/2016/10/06/3–how-americans-view-their-jobs/.

Phillips, Julie A., and Katherine Hempstead. "Differences in U.S. Suicide Rates by Educational Attainment. 2000–2014." *American Journal of Preventive Medicine* 53, no. 4 (2017). DOI:10.1016/j.amepre.2017.04.010.

Phillips, Katherine W. "How Diversity Makes Us Smarter." *Scientific American.* October 1, 2014. https://www.scientificamerican.com/article/how-diversity-makes-us-smarter/.

Rasmus, Carolyn J. "The Enabling Power of the Atonement." *Ensign.* March 2013. 18–21. https://media.ldscdn.org/pdf/magazines/ensign-march-2013/2013–03–07–the-enabling-power-of-the-atonement-eng. pdf?lang=eng.

Reeder, Jennifer, and Kate Holbrook (eds). *At the Pulpit: 185 Years of Discourse by Latter-Day Saint Women.* Salt Lake City: The Church Historian's Press, 2017.

Roosevelt, Eleanor. "10 Inspiring Quotes by Eleanor Roosevelt." *Virtues for Life.* Accessed August 2021. https://www.virtuesforlife.com/10-inspiring-quotes-by-eleanor-roosevelt

Ruiz, Rebecca. "America's Vainest Cities." *Forbes.* November 29, 2007. https://www.forbes.com/2007/11/29/plastic-health-surgery-forbeslife-cx_rr_1129health.html?sh=1c2a8a94decc.

Smith, Gordon T. *Courage and Calling: Embracing Your God-given Potential.* Downers Grove: InterVarsity Press, 2011.

Snow, Eliza R. *Poems, Religious, Historical, and Political, Vol. 1.* Liverpool: F. D. Richards, 1856. https://contentdm.lib.byu.edu/digital/collection/NCMP1820–1846/id/16773.

Starr, Michelle. "Sheryl Sandberg wants to ban the word 'bossy.'" *CNET.* March 10, 2014. https://www.cnet.com/news/sheryl-sandberg-wants-to-ban-the-word-bossy/.

Steger, Michael. F., Natalie K. Pickering, Joo Y. Shin, and Bryan J. Dik. "Calling in Work: Secular or Sacred?" *Journal of Career Assessment* 18, no. 1 (2010): 82–96. https://doi.org/10.1177/1069072709350905

Stephens, Carole M. "The Family is of God." *Liahona.* April 2015. https://media.ldscdn.org/pdf/magazines/liahona-may-2015/2015–05–00–liahona-eng.pdf?lang=eng.

Stevenson, Gary E. "Spiritual Eclipse." *Liahona.* November 2017. https://media.ldscdn.org/pdf/magazines/liahona-november-2017/2017–11–00–liahona-eng.pdf?lang=eng.

Tanner, Susan W. "The Sanctity of the Body." *Ensign.* November 2005. https://ia800409.us.archive.org/2/items/Ensign_Magazine-2005–11/Ensign_Magazine-2005–11.pdf.

Teachings of Presidents of the Church: Joseph F. Smith. Salt Lake City: The Church of Jesus Christ of Latter-day Saints, 1998. https://www.churchofjesuschrist.org/study/manual/teachings-joseph-f-smith.

Teresa, Mother and Brian Kolodiejchuk. *Mother Teresa: Come Be My light: The Private Writings of the Saint of Calcutta.* Manhattan: Crown Publishing, 2007. (From Mother Teresa's speech in Rome, March 7, 1979)

Tunheim, Katherine A., and Aimee N. Goldschmidt. "Exploring the Role of Calling in the Professional Journeys of College Presidents." *Journal of Leadership. Accountability and Ethics* 10, no. 4 (2013): 30–40.

Uchtdorf, Dieter F. "Living the Gospel Joyful." *General Conference.* October 2014. https://media.ldscdn.org/pdf/general-womens-session/september-2014–general-womens-session/2014–09–0050–president-dieter-f-uchtdorf-eng.pdf?lang=eng.

Uchtdorf, Dieter F. "You Matter to Him." *General Conference.* October 2011. https://media.ldscdn.org/pdf/general-conference/october-2011–general-conference/2011–10–1070–president-dieter-f-uchtdorf-eng.pdf?lang=eng.

Ulrich, Wendy. *Live Up to Our Privileges: Women, Power, and Priesthood.* Salt Lake City: Deseret Book, 2019.

Witesman, Eva M. "Women and Education: "A Future Only God Could See for You." *BYU Speeches.* June 27, 2017. https://speeches.byu.edu/wp-content/uploads/pdf/Witesman_Eva_2017–06–27B.pdf.

Woolley, Anita W., Christopher F. Chabris, Alexander Pentland, Nada Hashmi, and Thomas W. Malone. "Collective Intelligence: Number of Women in Group Linked to Effectiveness in Solving Difficult Problems." *Science Daily.* October 2, 2010. http://www.sciencedaily.com/releases/2010/09/100930143339.htm.

Yonker, Lael M., Shiyi Zan, Christina V. Scirica, Kamal Jethwani, and T. Bernard Kinane. "'Friending' Teens: Systematic Review of Social Media in Adolescent and Young Adult Health Care." *Journal of Medical Internet Research* 17, no. 1 (2015). https://doi.org/10.2196/jmir.3692.

Yousafzaim, Malala. "Quotable Quotes." *GoodReads.* https://www.goodreads.com/quotes/930638–when-the-whole-world-is-silent-even-one-voice-becomes

INDEX

ABOUT THE AUTHOR

Susan R. Madsen is the Karen Haight Huntsman Endowed Professor of Leadership in the Jon M. Huntsman School of Business at Utah State University. Dr. Madsen is considered one of the top global scholars and thought leaders on the topic of women and leadership and has authored or edited many books and hundreds of articles, chapters, and reports. She is a sought-after speaker in local, national, and international settings. Dr. Madsen, a returned missionary, received a bachelor's degree from BYU, master's from Portland State University, and a doctorate from the University of Minnesota. You can learn more about Susan's writings at www.susanrmadsen.com.

— NOTES —

— NOTES —

— NOTES —

— NOTES —

Scan to visit

http://www.afutureonlygodcanseeforyou.com/